U.S. Mint

Miscellaneous Letters Received from 1897 to 1903

Vol. 4

U.S. Mint

Miscellaneous Letters Received from 1897 to 1903
Vol. 4

ISBN/EAN: 9783337817176

Printed in Europe, USA, Canada, Australia, Japan

Cover: Foto ©Suzi / pixelio.de

More available books at **www.hansebooks.com**

RG 104, 8KRA-104-84-042
Box 2, Volume IV

Miscellaneous Letters Received,
1897-1903. Letters Received Relating
to the Construction of the New Denver
Mint, 1897-1906.

Washington,   May 23,1900.

The Superintendent of Construction,

    United States Mint,

        Denver, Colorado.

Sir:

    Referring to your letter of the 18th instant, addressed to the Supervising Architect, and referred to this Division, you are informed that one National Ensign, 4 1/4 X 8 feet, for use of your office, has been forwarded by today's mail to your address.

    You are requested to acknowledge the receipt of same.

        Respectfully,

        Acting Chief of Division.

DENVER MINT.

TREASURY DEPARTMENT
OFFICE OF THE SUPERVISING ARCHITECT

Washington, **May 23, 1900.**

Superintendent of Construction,

New Mint Building,

Denver, Colorado.

Sir:-

I have to acknowledge the receipt of your letter of the 17th instant, in which you call attention to the fact that the bead on the shaft of certain columns at the building in your charge has been broken, and in which you desire to know whether permission will be given to reduce the size of the columns in order to obtain the bead on the shaft, or to take the bead off from the shaft and cut it on the capitals.

Favorable consideration cannot be given to reducing the size of the columns. If, however, the contractor submits a proposal to cut the bead on the capital so as to make the joint below the bead, without expense to the Government, it is probable that it will receive favorable consideration.

Respectfully,

Supervising Architect.

J.G.

Printed Heading.

Denver,Colo.,May 28th,1900.

Lee Ullery,Esq.,

      Superintendent of Construction,

           New Mint, Denver, Colo.

Sir:-

      Replying to your favor May 26th, I have the honor to
submit for the consideration of the Department, the following
proposition:

      I will cut bead on capital so as to make joint below the
bead for all center columns found defective without cost to the
United States.

           Very respectfully,

                (Signed) J.A.McIntyre,
                          T.

The Superintendent of Janstruc

United States (New) Mint,

TREASURY DEPARTMENT

OFFICE OF THE SECRETARY

In reply to this Letter the
order herewith quoted and
consecutive be referred to.

(TELEGRAM)

Washington, June 5,1900.

John A. McIntyre,

Cooper Building,

Denver, Colorado.

Tardy progress under your contract Denver Mint unsatisfactory,
unbusinesslike and will not be tolerated. Decided measures
will be taken by Department.

(Signed) H. A. Taylor,
Assistant Secretary.

Official business,
Government rates,
Charge Treasury.

(Signed) J. K. Taylor,
Supervising Architect.

TREASURY DEPARTMENT

OFFICE OF THE **SECRETARY.**

Washington,   June 5,1900.

(C O P Y)

The U.S.Fidelity & Guaranty Company,
          Baltimore,
                    Maryland.

Gentlemen:

Referring to Department letter of September 20th last and to previous communications of similar tenor addressed to you as sureties on bond given by Mr.John A. McIntyre,in connection with his contract for the foundation,superstructure and roof covering,etc.,at the United States Mint Building,Denver,Colorado,you are now informed that the conditions looking to completion of the work at an early date remain practically as then stated,with the exception that a larger portion of material has been delivered.

Enclosed find copy of Department telegram this day addressed to the contractor.

A fair delivery of material has been made on the ground but the force employed in setting same in place is most inadequate. It is necessary also that delivery be made at once of all granite requisite to the completion of that branch of the work. The conditions are favorable to hauling at this season of the year.

Respectfully,

(Signed) H. A. Taylor,

Assistant Secretary.

VBV.

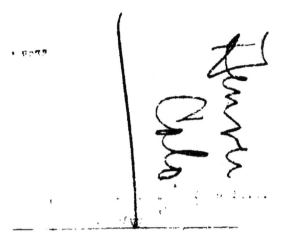

DENVER,COLO. Mint (new)

Enclosure.

In replying to this letter the
initials in upper right-hand
corner must be referred to.

TREASURY DEPARTMENT

OFFICE OF THE SUPERVISING ARCHITECT

Washington, June 7, 1900.

The Superintendent of Construction,
    New Mint Building,
        Denver, Colorado.

Sir:-

   I enclose herewith, for your information and the files of
your office, a copy of Department letter of even date, accepting the proposition-forwarded in your letter of the 28th ultimo-
of Mr. J.A.McIntyre, the contractor for the superstructure,etc.
of the building in your charge, to cut bead on capital,so as
to make joint below the bead, for all center columns found defective, without additional cost to the Government, all as
stated in the said letter of acceptance.

                    Respectfully,

                    Supervising Architect.

J.S.S.

DENVER, COLORADO: NEW MINT.

TREASURY DEPARTMENT

OFFICE OF THE SUPERVISING ARCHITECT

Washington, **June 6, 1900.**

The Superintendent of Construction,

    United States (new) Mint,

        Denver, Colorado.

Sir:

    I am in receipt of your letter of the 10th ultimo
relative to the fireproofing of the girders for the
building under your charge, and in reply I have to advise you that the files of this office do not show
that sketches for this work have ever been submitted
for approval. I have therefore to request that you
instruct the contractor accordingly and require him
to forward same at once.

        Respectfully,

                    Supervising Architect.

R.

DENVER COLO. New Mint.

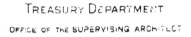

TREASURY DEPARTMENT

OFFICE OF THE SUPERVISING ARCHITECT

Washington, June 9, 1900.

The Superintendent of Construction,
        New Mint Building,
                Denver, Colorado.

Sir:-

    I have to acknowledge the receipt of your letter of the
22d ultimo, and, under separate cover, sample of Red Diamond
Portland cement, taken from the material delivered by the contractor for the building in your charge.

    Tests of the said sample show that the cement is satis-
factory.

                Respectfully,

                        Supervising Architect.

J.S.S.

DENVER MINT.

TREASURY DEPARTMENT

OFFICE OF THE SUPERVISING ARCHITECT

Washington,   June 13, 1900.

Superintendent of Construction,

    New Mint Building,

        Denver, Colorado.

Sir:-

    I have to acknowledge the receipt of your letter of the
22nd ultimo, relative to certain galvanized iron flue linings
included in the contract of Mr. J. A. McIntyre for the foundations, superstructure, etc., of the building in your charge.

    In preparing the final plans for heating and ventilating
apparatus, it has been found advisable to modify certain portions
of the original arrangement, and in order to simplify the same
you are requested to obtain a proposal from the contractor for
the omission of the galvanized iron flue referred to in your
above mentioned letter, and of its terra cotta enclosure, and
if such proposal is one which can be accepted, the flue in its
modified form will be provided for under the contract for the
heating apparatus. Please forward the proposal as soon as
possible with your definite recommendation.

            Respectfully,

                        Supervising Architect.

J.G.

TREASURY DEPARTMENT

OFFICE OF THE SUPERVISING ARCHITECT

Washington,   June 15, 1900.

Enclosure.

Mr. Lee Ullery,

    Superintendent of Construction,

        Mint Building, Denver, Colorado.

Sir:-

    I return herewith voucher, in duplicate, approved upon its face, drawn in your favor, in the sum of..............$11.05, for expenses incurred by you in traveling from Denver to Arkins, Colorado, and return, under orders from this Department, for presentation to the Disbursing Agent of the building in your charge, for payment from funds in his hands appropriated for "Mint Building, Denver, Colorado," as per instructions this day given.

        Respectfully,

                Jas. A. Wetmore.
                Acting Chief Executive Officer.

F.D.

Superintendent of Construction,
U. S. Mint (New),
Denver, Colorado.

Sir:

I have to direct that you will, on the last day of the present month, prepare and mail a letter addressed to this office, giving briefly but explicitly the following information:

FIRST.   The point of advancement of each branch of the work at June 30th, 1900, and,

SECOND,   A brief synopsis of the work accomplished in the period between June 30th, 1899 (date of last report) and June 30th, 1900.

It should be noted that quantities are not desired, but the statement should be prepared in such manner as will convey readily the condition of the work, for use in connection with the preparation of the annual report of the operations on buildings under the control of this office, under date of June 30th, 1900.

Should the advancement since date of last photograph be such as to warrant securing new views you are directed to submit an estimate of the cost of securing photographic views of the building in accordance with the spirit of Section VIII of printed "Instructions to Superintendents". In order that if so desired, proper departmental action may be taken authorizing you to incur a liability for obtaining views of the building, each negative to have scratched in the lower left hand corner, on the film side of the negative, the title and location of the building and date, which must be June 30th, 1900.

Respectfully,

Acting Supervising Architect.

class of C

Mrs. New,

Dexter, C

send boxes

Melbourne

TREASURY DEPARTMENT

OFFICE OF THE SECRETARY

Washington,   June 16, 1900.

S

Mr.John A.McIntyre,

    Rooms 403-404 Cooper Building,

      Denver, Colorado.

Sir:

    Acknowledgment is hereby made of your letter of the 6th instant,
complaining of the treatment received by you from the Superintendent
of Construction at the U.S.Mint (new), Denver, Colorado, in connection
with your contract for the erection of the building.

    The statements made by you have been noted, and in reply, you are
advised that the Department has every reason to believe that the officer named is not requiring the performance of any work, nor the supply
of any material not fully provided for by the terms of the contract.

    When you submitted your proposal for the work indicated, and an
acceptance was made thereof, and you entered into a contract for the
faithful and satisfactory completion thereof, it was fair to presume
that you had full knowledge of all the conditions imposed thereby and
had perfected your arrangements to carry out the terms of the agreement.

    It is apparent, however, that the present backward condition of
the work is essentially due to the fact that you are not employing the
necessary force of workmen; that the arrangements at the quarry for the
shipment of the granite are crude, incomplete and unsatisfactory, and
also that you have failed to adopt proper businesslike methods.

You are now directed, therefore, to proceed to secure the delivery
of all material complete, with the exception of granite for the upper
member of the main cornice, now receiving consideration as to changing
the material, and to advance the work with greater dispatch.   Should
you insist upon placing in the building any material, which in finish
and character is not in reasonable compliance with the terms of the a-
greement, you must understand that you do so at your own risk.

In this connection, you are informed that a representative of this
Department will visit Denver early in July to confer with the Superintendent of Construction and with you, to report the point of advancement
reached, and to determine whether you have supplied material, either in
character or finish, in violation of the terms of the specifications
and drawings.   The representative referred to will be required to submit a report in writing, and upon its receipt, the Department will give
consideration thereto and base its action thereon, as to the adoption
of such measures as may be necessary for the protection of the Government's interests.

A copy of this letter has been forwarded to the Superintendent of
Construction, with necessary instructions in line with this communication.

                              Respectfully,

                              (Signed) H.A.Taylor
                              Assistant Secretary.

E.
7.

DENVER, COLORADO: NEW MINT.

In replying to this Letter the
initials in upper right-hand
corner must be referred to.

TREASURY DEPARTMENT
OFFICE OF THE SUPERVISING ARCHITECT

Washington, June 22, 1900.

The Superintendent of Construction,

United States (new) Mint,

Denver, Colorado.

Sir:

I am in receipt of your letter of the 16th instant
and the copy of City Ordinance No. 24, series of 1900, therein referred to, which will be utilized in the preparation
of the approach plans for the building under your charge.

Respectfully,

Supervising Architect.

R.

15

5

Treasury Department,

OFFICE OF THE SUPERVISING ARCHITECT,

Washington, D. C., June 21, 1900.

Superintendent of Construction,

    Mint Building (new),

        Denver, Colorado.

Sir:

In view of the request and recommendation contained in your letter of the 16th instant and the public exigency requiring the immediate delivery of the articles and performance of the work you are hereby authorized to incur an expenditure not exceeding five dollars ($5,00)

in securing in open market at lowest prevailing rates:

photographic views of work on the building, $5.00

Your attention is called to printed "Instructions to Superintendents," and you will issue and certify vouchers on account of the above in accordance therewith, payment to be made from the appropriation for "Mint Building, Denver, Colo."

Respectfully yours,

Chief Executive Officer.

Form No. 108.

THE WESTERN UNION TELEGRAPH COMPANY.
—— INCORPORATED ——
21,000 OFFICES IN AMERICA.   CABLE SERVICE TO ALL THE WORLD.

This Company TRANSMITS and DELIVERS messages only on conditions limiting its liability, which have been assented to by the sender of the following message.
Errors can be guarded against only by repeating a message back to the sending station for comparison, and the Company will not hold itself liable for errors or delays
in transmission or delivery of Unrepeated Messages, beyond the amount of tolls paid thereon, nor in any case where the claim is not presented in writing within sixty days
after the message is filed with the Company for transmission.
This is an UNREPEATED MESSAGE, and is delivered by request of the sender, under the conditions named above.

330

THOS. T. ECKERT, President and General Manager.

RECEIVED at 1114 to 1118 17th St., Denver, Colo.   Standard Time.

14 A Nt Fo 36 Paid. Govt.

Washington D C June 25-00

Superintendent Ullery New Mint Denver, Colo.

McIntyres representative requested favorable consideration
of proposition to furnish Platte
Canon granite for cornice proposition
in writing has not been
received. Look it up, reply.

J K Taylor, Supervising Architect

820a .m.

JOHN A. McINTYRE,
GENERAL CONTRACTOR,
ROOMS 402-404 COOPER BUILDING,
DENVER, COLO.
Telephone 1258.

OWNER AND OPERATOR
ARKINS GRANITE QUARRIES.

18

Denver Coloeado, June 26 1900.

Lee Ullery Supt.

U. S. Mint (new)

Denver Colorado.

Sir.

I have the honor to acknowledge receipt of your
letter June 25th, authorizing change in jointing of ashlar for
chimney and vent stacks by cutting the neck mould on the course
below.

Very Respectfully.

JOHN A. McINTYRE,
GENERAL CONTRACTOR,
ROOMS 402-404 COOPER BUILDING,
DENVER, COLO.
Telephone 1238.

OWNER AND OPERATOR
ARKINS GRANITE QUARRIES.

Denver Colorado, June 26 1900.

Lee Ulley Supt.

U. S. Mint (new)

Denver Colorado.

Sir.

Acknowledging receipt of your letter June 16th. inst. requesting proposition for the omission of 6' x 1' hot air flue between columns No. 10 & 11 in the U. S. Mint (new) under my contract, I have the honor to ask of said omission is required through any fault or over sight of mine, and if so to advise you of my willingness to at once rectify said error in conformity with your directions.

Very Respectfully.

JOHN A. McINTYRE,
GENERAL CONTRACTOR,
ROOMS 402-404 COOPER BUILDING,
DENVER, COLO.
Telephone 1238.

OWNER AND OPERATOR
ARKINS GRANITE QUARRIES.

secure acceptable Colorado stone, I have wired the Supervising

Architect, asking if he would entertain a proposition for the

use of eastern grey granite similar in color and texture to

that now in use in the building, and should he be pleased to do

so, I will at once submit through your office a proposition

for such substitution.

Very Respectfully.

John A. McIntyre

TREASURY DEPARTMENT
OFFICE OF THE SUPERVISING ARCHITECT

Washington, July 3,1900.

Superintendent of Construction,

U.S.Mint (New),

Denver, Colorado.

Sir:

Under date of the 23rd ultimo the Custodian of the U.S.Post-Office and Court-House building, at Denver, Colorado, submits a request from the Local Forecast Official, &c., Weather Bureau service, for the erection of a plastered partition in their office on the fifth floor (tower) of the building, and also the cutting of ventilators in the ceiling of each room.

You are requested to give these features your attention, to prepare specifications for such work as may be necessary in connection therewith, and to forward your report, with such suggestions or recommendations as the Government's interests would seem to demand, with an estimate of the probable cost involved, for further action.

Respectfully,

Supervising Architect.

Denver,Colo.,July 5th,1900.

Lee Ullery, Supt.,

U.S.Mint (New),

Denver, Colorado.

Sir:-

Replying to your letter June 27th ,ulto, relating to omission of hot air flue I have the honor to say,that inasmuch as most of the material required for this construction has been delivered and the lining itself cut and manufactured, I cannot see my way to a proposition contemplating any deduction from the contract price allowed for the said work.

Regretting my inability to meet your wishes in this matter I am

Very respectfully,

J.A.McIntyre,
T.

Division of Stationery, Printing, and Blanks.

Form
(Ed. 7-6-'97—3,000.)

Treasury Department,

OFFICE OF THE SECRETARY,

July 6, 1900

Sir:

Your requisition of _____ for stationery has been received, and will be filed as soon as possible. It must be borne in mind that the Public Printer requires two months' time in which to print paper and envelopes.

Respectfully yours,

George Simmons

Chief of Division of Stationery, Printing, and Blanks.

Per _____

2—75

Treasury Department,

OFFICE OF THE SECRETARY.

July 6, 190 0.

Sir:

In your requisition of June 30 you called for typewriter ribbons but failed to specify the kind of machine used in your office. It will be necessary for you to furnish this information before they can be supplied. Respectfully,

CHIEF OF DIVISION OF STATIONERY, PRINTING, AND BLANKS.

UNITED STATES Mint

Superintendent of Construc
New Mint Building
(?)

Sir:

I have to acknowledge the
of nothing, in which you refe
letter of May 24,19(?) relati
building in your charge.

It has been the intention
picture installed in the north
more detail (?), at the sa
in connection with the floor,

As it is understood from
statement (?) fan to permit of
stating extra expense it has b
ranged as now (followed) to t
re (?) an to see building

DENVER MINT

Enclosure.

TREASURY DEPARTMENT

OFFICE OF THE SUPERVISING ARCHITECT

Washington, **July 12, 1900.**

In reply to this letter the within in upper right-hand corner must be referred to.

The Superintendent of Construction,
    New Mint Building,
       Denver, Colorado.

Sir:-

    This Office is in receipt of a letter dated the 9th instant from Mr. John A. McIntyre, the contractor for the superstructure of the building in your charge, with enclosures, relative to certain material which has been rejected by you, which papers are forwarded herewith.

    Please give the matter consideration and report your views to this Office at once, with your definite recommendation, returning, at the same time, the papers in question.

        Respectfully,

               Supervising Architect.

J.S.S.

PRINTED HEADING.

Denver,Colorado, July 9,1900.

Hon.J.K.Taylor,
    Supervising Architect,
      Washington, D.C.

Sir:-

      On March 27th,1900, I received from the Celadon Terra
Cotta Co.,under their sub-contract for the roofing tile for use in
the U.S.Mint New) four (4) Corner Finials of special design as called for the by the plans and specification for said building. These
finials were in my opinion,of perfect manufacture and material,and
were well within the requirements of your specifications,but in order to avoid delay at a subsequent date, my foreman (acting under
my order) submitted the said finials to your Superintendent of Construction for his approval.

      On June 18,after the receipt of one additional finial,to
replace one broken in transit,Mr.Ullery directed that I advise The
Celadon Terra Cotta Co. as follows:

      " x x x x x corner finials furnished by you are not vit-
rified as called for in the specifications,they being coated on the
outside with what appears to be a coat of paint or similar material,
whereas the color should be obtained by burning to vitrification,
producing a uniform color and texture throughout; You will remedy
this condition at once,either by removing or reburning the same,as
required in the case of hip rolls heretofore mentioned. x x x x"

      I have the honor to now lay before you the original letters
this day received from the Celadon Terra Cotta Co. and the American
Terra Cotta & Ceramic Co. relating to said finials.

      I feel at liberty to refer to you in this matter,and ask
to be relieved from this situation if we are right,as I feel that we
are.

      Just such continual differences are what has caused much of
the delay heretofore existing on the work,and I feel that such will
continue to be the case.

      Trusting for your approval of the materials in question, I
am

           Very respectfully,

               J.A.MCINTYRE.

Chicago, Ill., July 6, 1900.

Mr. J. A. McIntyre,
      402 Cooper Building,
         Denver, Colorado.

Dear Sir:-

    We have asked our Denver agents, the Golden Pressed Brick and Fire Brick Co., to remove the loo pieces of Hip Roll, which were considered by the Superintendent of the U.S. Mint Building as being too soft for use. On May 26th we shipped from our Ottawa factory an additional loo pieces of Hip Roll to replace the ones which were not up to the requirements of the Department.

    In answer to your comment upon the Corner Finials furnished, we will call your attention to the enclosed letter from the manufacturers of this material. We have not made terra cotta at our factory for some time, having turned our attention entirely to the manufacture of roofing tile, and in order that we might give you very high grade and satisfactory material we had the Corner Finials made by the American Terra Cotta & Ceramic Co of this city, who are one of the highest grade terra cotta manufacturers in the country. You will notice that the body of all kinds of terra cotta ware is composed of various kinds and qualities of clay. This is done to make a strong and firm body, one that will be durable and retain its shape, and in order to get the color it is necessary to semi-glaze the outer surface. This is done not only by this Company, but by every other terra cotta manufacturer in the United States, and no terra cotta ware is furnished, either to the Government or any body else, which has not been treated in the same way. The process is practical and we trust you will find the material satisfactory for your use, with the assurance from the manufacturers that it is as good as the best.

                Yours truly

                        Celadon Roofing Tile Co.,
                            E. J. Hess,
                            Ass't Sec'y & Treas.

Dic. EJH-O
enc.

Celadon Roofing Tile Company,
         Marquette Building, Chicago.

Gentlemen:-

          In answer to yours of the 27th instant containing ex-
tract from your letter from a general contractor, stating that the
finials furnished by us were not vitrified and were coated on the
outside with what he considers paint, I would say that it is well
recognized among clay workers that no large piece of vitrified
piece of clay ware can be produced with anything at all like a
straight line.

          In making large pieces it is absolutely necessary to use
a carefully mixed body, having a proper proportion of calcined fire
clay to hold it up. This is done in all our ware, and this is by
no means the first instance of our having furnished material to the
Government of like character.

          What he is pleased to term "paint" is a carefully prepar-
ed solution of clay applied to the surface of the ware before burning, and which in the process of burning fuses in making a skin like
surface impervious to moisture.

          Such finials as he has there could never be produced with
a vitrified body all the way through, and even making them as we have
made them, so large and thin are they, we had to make them over several times. We cannot make better ones, nor can better ones be produced anywhere. Of this we are confident.

                         Very respectfully,

                         THE AMERICAN TERRA COTTA COMPANY,
                              H.B.PROSSER

                                   SECRETARY.

Treasury Department,

OFFICE OF THE SUPERVISING ARCHITECT,

Washington, D. C.,   **July 13, 1900.**

Mr. **Lee Ullery,**

Supt. U. S. **MINT,**

Denver, Col.

Sir :

I have to acknowledge the receipt of your "*Estimate of Funds*" required for the work on the building under your superintendence during **the month of July, 1900,** 189–, and to advise you that, as it appears the remittance of funds heretofore made to the Disbursing Agent on account of the appropriation for the building is sufficient to meet all vouchers issued or to be issued for expenditures on account of the work on the building, to and including the last day of the current month, no further remittance will be made to him at present.

Respectfully, yours,

Acting ⟨signature⟩

Chief Executive Officer.

Form 32.
d. 12-29-'94—2,000.

Cotopaxi July 16th 1900

Lee Ullery Esq

Dear Sir

I send you today by
mail a small sample of Pink Granite
which I can furnish if desired as
a substitute for the Arkins stone
for the Cornice for the Mint building

Very Respectfully Yours

F. L. Gilman

P.S. Quantity
unlimited G

DENVER MINT.

32

TREASURY DEPARTMENT

OFFICE OF THE SUPERVISING ARCHITECT

Washington, July 14, 1900.

Superintendent of Construction,

New Mint Building,

Denver, Colorado.

Sir:-

I have to acknowledge the receipt of your letter of the 9th instant, enclosing proposal for omission of certain galvanized iron flue lining and terra cotta enclosure for the same in the building in your charge.

Inasmuch as no deduction will be allowed for such omission, you are directed to instruct the contractor to place the flue and enclosure referred to, in accordance with his original contract.

Respectfully,

Supervising Architect.

J.G.

Hon. Harry Rny.

U.S. Commissioner,

United States Mint, New

Dear Sir:

I was this morning notified by the Adams Express
Company that the packages containing bars from P. F.
Taylor & Co. Children, and consigned to me, would be received in
the silver yards July 10th.

Presuming that this completed the remainder of the shipment
for the Denver Mint I prepared to have same placed on the site
although as my act informed you of the arrival.

Mr. L. F. McGready of Taylor, Bros. has asked that no more P. M.
and informs me that there will be available no supplies for the site but
is loaded with a extra settled supplies, and that the matter required
for the production of the Mint will come as shipped from Chicago
but the larger part of such here.

Sincerely regretting this delay, which was caused in some mall
by late troubles and

Very respectfully,

Jasmhtzr

DENVER. NEW MINT.

B

In reply the mistake in the letter the match the in upper right hand corner must be referred to.

TREASURY DEPARTMENT
OFFICE OF THE SUPERVISING ARCHITECT

Washington, **July 20,1900.**

Enclosure.

Superintendent of Construction,

U. S. Mint (new),

Denver, Colorado.

Sir:

For your information find copy of Department letter of the 18th instant, addressed to Mr. John A. McIntyre, contractor for the erection of the superstructure of the building under your charge, in relation to progress of work.

Respectfully,

Supervising Architect.

TREASURY DEPARTMENT

OFFICE OF THE SECRETARY

Washington, **July 18, 1900.**

Mr. John A. McIntyre,

    402 Cooper Building,

        Denver, Colorado.

Sir:

    Your letter of the 28th ultimo is hereby acknowledged, in relation to the progress of work under contract with you for the erection of the U. S. Mint building, Denver, Colorado.

    The statements made are duly noted, and you are informed that this Department has every reason to believe that the Superintendent of Construction, who is under bond to faithfully guard the interests of the Government, has not demanded from you the performance of any work not clearly provided for in the agreement.

    The delays which have been encountered are such as could have been controlled and removed had you exercised proper businesslike methods, the adoption of which should have been prompted by a due consideration of the interests of your bondsmen.

    The main question now, it is understood, looking to the completion of the work at no remote day, is one which affects the material to be used in the main cornice of the building.

that there are obstructions in the way of securing from the
Arkins Quarry stones of dimensions required by the drawings
for the cornice, but intimation has been so given to the
Office of the Supervising Architect.

You must recognize that the contract cannot be modified
except by the consent of the two contracting parties, and
should you desire that consideration be given to the substitution of some granite other than that from the Arkins Quarry
for use in the cornice, you should submit such request in
writing, with the full understanding that no expense shall
be entailed upon the Government in the event of consent being
given.

Mr. John A. Dewees, representing you, lately called
at the Office of the Supervising Architect of this Department,
and intimated that enquiries were being made with the view of
submitting a proposition from you, which, however, at this
date has not been presented.

Under date of the 6th ultimo, in a telegram addressed
to the Supervising Architect of this Department, you stated
that you would make important showing to Department "by per-
sonal representative as to present condition and future
progress of this contract".

Shortly subsequent to the receipt of said telegram,
Mr. Charles Hartwell called at the Office of the Supervising
Architect.   Mr. Hartwell at the time, and subsequent to the
acceptance of your proposal for the work, has acted as your

counsel, duly authorized to treat for you.   He requested
that consideration be given to the substitution of some other
granite than that from Arkins Quarry in the cornice, and alleged that it could be secured without difficulty and with
dispatch and assured the Supervising Architect that if such
permission was granted the building would be under roof within
ninety days thereafter.   Mr. Hartzell concluded with the
assurance that he would return to Denver and secure from you
a proposition in writing presenting the matter to the Department for consideration, accompanied by a request for favorable
action, and you are informed that the Department is prepared
to give such proposition due consideration provided that the
same is presented without further delay.

In this connection also it is proper to state that
Mr. Hartzell, during his visit referred to, spoke to the
Supervising Architect in the highest terms of the Superintendent of Construction at the building, and alleged that
he had been impartial and reasonable in interpreting the requirements of the contract, and had given advice concerning
the work which had been of value to the contractor and the
other interests involved in this matter.

You are now requested to give this matter your immediate attention, in order that the work can be completed
without further vexatious delay.

Respectfully,

F.

T.   (Signed) H. A. Taylor
                              Assistant Secretary.

SOP   G. H. S.

Envelope to
Supt. of Construction
U. S. Mint (new),
Denver, Colo.

Denver,Colo.U.S.Mint,Const.St.No.

TREASURY DEPARTMENT

OFFICE OF THE SUPERVISING ARCHITECT

Washington   July 24,1902.

Superintendent of Construction,

    U.S.Mint,

        Denver ,Colorado.

   Sir:-

      Your letter of the 19th instant was duly received,enclosing
specification for partitions,etc.,in the Weather Bureau Office in
the tower of the Court House and Post Office building in your city,
the work being estimated to cost four hundred dollars ($400.00).

      The specification is approved and you are authorized to take
competitive bids for the performance of the work,forwarding them
through the Custodian of the building with your recommendation as to
acceptance.

                    Respectfully,

                    Acting Supervising Architect.

37
206

July 24,1900.

The Superintendent of Construction,

United States (New) Mint,

Denver, Colorado.

Sir:

I am in receipt of your letter of the 17th instant relative the flue lining passing between certain beams in the building under your charge,and in reply I have to advise you that said flue should be constructed according to the drawings,making the necessary constriction in same to pass beams without cutting flanges thereof.

Respectfully,

Acting Supervising Architect.

TREASURY DEPARTMENT

Melbourne.

Treasury Department,

Office of the Secretary August 2,1900.

Washington, D. C.,

Mr. John A. McIntyre,
    Cooper Building,
        Denver, Colorado.

Sir:-

Your proposition, dated the 18th ultimo, addressed to
the Supervising Architect of this Department ,is hereby accepted
to substitute Maine grey granite, from Davidson Bros. Quarry,
for the top member of the cornice of the new Mint Building at
Denver, Colorado, in lieu of the stone being used in the building, without additional cost to the Government under your contract for the foundation, superstructure and roof covering,for
which your original proposal was accepted March 29.1898, this
action being taken in view of the difficulty in obtaining
stone of the proper size for this member of the cornice from
the quarry furnishing the stone approved for use in the work.

It is understood and agreed that this substitution is not
to affect the time for the completion of the work as required
by the terms of your contract;that the same is without prejudice to any and all rights of the United States thereunder;and
without prejudice,also, to any and all rights of the United
States against the sureties on the bond executed for the faithful fulfillment of the contract.

A sample of the approved granite from the quarry of Davidson Bros.,has been forwarded to the superintendent of the build-

ing,for the files of his office and his guidance in accepting
the material for this portion of the work .

Please promptly acknowledge the receipt of this letter,
a copy of which will be forwarded to the superintendent.

Respectfully,

J.C.P.   Secretary.

J.S.B.

DENVER. NEW MINT.

B

*In replying to this Letter the
initials in upper right-hand
corner must be referred to.*

Enclosure.

TREASURY DEPARTMENT
OFFICE OF THE SUPERVISING ARCHITECT

Washington, August 3, 1900.

Superintendent of Construction,

    U. S. Mint (New),

        Denver, Colorado.

Sir:

      Referring to previous correspondence and to all the circumstances attending the prosecution of work under a contract with John A. McIntyre and Company, for the erection of the superstructure, including roof and covering, of the building under your charge, find now enclosed copy of report dated the 23rd ultimo, submitted by Mr. A. A. Packard, Inspector of Public Buildings, as the result of an examination made by him of the work.

      The report is enclosed for your information and guidance and your attention is especially called to the statement made to the Inspector by the contractors that they would immediately increase the force of cutters at the yard and that every effort would be made to expedite the prosecution and secure early completion of the work.

      The matter of terra cotta floor arches has, it is believed, already received your consideration and it is understood that you have informed the contractors that building of the arches was at their own risk and that they would be held to strict responsibility as to the integrity and good character of the work. In this connection your attention is called to page D of the specification forming part of the contract, providing for tests of arches at the expense of the contractors and you are requested to outline a method for such tests and to

submit to this office for approval, conveying definite information
as to when the tests can be made.

You have been informed as to the action of the Department in
assenting to a modification of the contract by permitting the use of
New England granite in lieu of Platte canon in crown member of main
cornice and you are requested to ascertain from the contractors as to
the probable date when complete delivery will be made thereof and also
as to whether the same will be delivered cut lewised and ready for
setting.

This office recognizes the services rendered by you, and in the
event that no vital interests are involved, you are requested to take
such steps as may be necessary looking to the securing of the completion of the work at the earliest date.

Respectfully,

Supervising Architect.

ARCHITECTURAL INSPECTOR OF

PUBLIC BUILDINGS

Denver, Colo., July 23,1900

Supervising Architect,

Washington,D.C.

Sir:-

In accordance with instructions in Department Letter
of July 12,1900, I visited and inspected the new Mint Building in
Denver, Colo., and acquired into the conditions relative to the
work performed, under a contract with J.A.McIntyre & Co., of
Denver, for the erection of the superstructure, steel, stone and
roof covering.

I found the work
At the time of my visit July 19th-23rd completed and
in course of erection as follows: In the basement all sewer work
is complete except an outside manhole; all walls and partitions
practically finished - except area walls and walls for coal
vault and the fire proofing around some of the columns.

On the first floor all of the terra cotta floor arches and
the brick floor arches are in place and most of the terra cotta
partitions are up to the height of the mezzanine floor. On the
second floor, the central portion of the terra cotta floor arches
is in place; all of the heating and ventilating ducts are in, or
in place to be put in; all of the structural steel in the building
proper is in place, except a few beams for the attic floor, which
cannot be put in until the wall is finished. All of the steel
work for the roof is on the ground and work on its erection will

be commenced at the earliest possible moment, which ought not
to be later than Sept. 10,1900. All of the tile roofing material
is on the ground and nearly all of the hip rolls and finials and
there should be no delay in placing this material when the steel
work is ready for it. The balance of the terra cotta floor arches
and partitions has not been delivered yet but I understand it can
be delivered at the building on short notice. There are still
some 18 pieces of marble lacking, mostly caps, and arches which
are short on account of defects in some material already delivered.
These pieces of marble are promised in two weeks.

The granite stone work has progressed as follows: All
of the work on the East end is completed, up to the xxxxx top or
crown mould course, which I understand is to be procured from the
East. On the north side the corners are up to the top, or crown
mould course and the central portion up to just above the spring
line of the second floor arches. Some of the stone is ready
for the work but waiting for the marble arches which have been
promised in two weeks. On the west side the corners are complete
up to crown mould course and the remaining portion up to the
second story arches. On the south side the corners are on up
to the crown mould course, and about one-half of the central
portion is ready for the cornice proper, and the other half about
two courses below. There are still about eighty-five pieces of
stone lacking for the building proper- not including the top
crown course to come from the East - or the stone for chimneys,
coping and retaining wall and most of the material for these

eighty five pieces has been quarried and is waiting to be delivered
at the yards and out and with the present force of men at work
at the yards,-(sixty two,- at the time of my visit) it will
probably take from six weeks to two months to finish and set all
of this work. From the material I saw on hand, I think more
men could be worked at the cutting to advantage - but after
having a conference with the contractor, I find that he is having
considerable difficulty in getting men, - on account of labor
difficulties - but he had a settlement of one of his difficulties
at the time of my visit, and he informed me he would put on more
men if he could get them and work them to advantage.

As I understand the material for the crown mould course
is to come from the East and also to be cut in the East, I see
no reason why there should be any more delay in regard to
furnishing and setting the balance of the stone. I did not visit
the quarry from which the present stone is being furnished I -
but I understand, both from the Supterintendent of Construction
and Contractor, that enough for finishing the job has been opened
up - about which there will be no question as to its meeting
with the requirements of the specifications.

In regard to the quality of the work and material
supplied - I will state that it is an unusually good job of
work in all respects, both as to materials supplied and workmanship
performed. The only thing I can find fault with is the terra

cotta floor arches - some of the portions which have been put in
appear very soft and in bad condition generally - whether this
is from exposure to the weather or from faulty manufacture -
I am unable to determine, although it appears to me there is a
little of both . These floors of course should not be put in
until they can be protected from the weather - the contracter
did so, however, at his own risk. I would recommend thatall of
these floor arches be gone over thoroughly and such as show any
defect at all be taken out and replaced by new sound material
and that this work and the remaining floor work shall not be done
until the building is under cover. The terra cotta work in the
tile partitions seems to be of better quality of material and
such as are in place are all right.

The granite work is of excellent quality and harmonious
color and the cutting and carving is as near perfect as can be
obtained and aside from the delays, I think the Superintendent
of Construction is obtaining work and material in even more than
fair harmony with the terms of the contract. As to whether the
methods adopted by him are such as may be reasonably expected of
one charged with responsibility of properly protecting the
Government's interests in securing the performance of work under
contract - I will state that after a careful examination and
conference with him in regard to several matters, my impression
and thoughtful opinion is that in some instances he has possibly
drawn the line too fine and has interpreted the specifications too

literally and not quite in the spirit in which I infer they are
to be taken and in harmony with good commercial usage. I will
also add that I think he has been thoroughly conscientious and
honest in all his decisions and has endeavored to the best of his
ability to protect the Government's interests in all respects.
Lately, I think he has been broader with his interpretation of
specifications and I tried to impress him with the fact that I
did not think the Government required literal technical interpretation of all specifications - but more the spirit of good work.
I do not think there will be any more trouble or delay on this
account - and my only recommendation is that the interpretation of
specification and drawings be not too technical or literal but
a more liberal spirit in harmony with good commercial usage by
employed.

I spent considerable time in enquiring into and investigat-
ing the conditions relative to the cause of delay and trouble in
connection with this contract and I have obtained information from
several reliable disinterested parties which may be of use to
the Department when the final settlement is made with Mr.McIntyre.

Respectfully,

Chicago, Ill.,August 7th,1900.

Mr.J.A.McIntyre,

    402 Cooper Building, Denver, Colorado.

Dear Sir:-

    Replying to your favor of the 27th ult. we enclose to you
a copy of letter this day received from the American Terra Cotta Co.
who made for us the corner block finials for the U.S.Mint building.
Inasmuch as this Company is not a party in any way to your contract,
we wish to repeat what they say,assuming on behalf of our company
their guaranty as follows:

    We will fully guarantee that the surface coating of the cor-
ner block finials furnished by us for the U.S.Mint building are slip-
ped coatings burned into the ware,and are absolutely durable;that the
color is permanent and that should these pieces show any defects within the next five (5) years in the material or coloring matter,we will
remove and replace these finials with such as shall be satisfactory
without expense to the Government.

                        Yours very respectfully,

                            Celadon Roofing Tile Company

                                Henry S.Harris,
                                    Vice-President.

Denver,Colo.,August 13th,1900.

Lee Ullery,Esq.,

      Supt.Construction U.S.Mint building,

          Denver, Colorado.

Sir:-

      I have the honor to acknowledge the receipt of your letter
August 6th,1900,relating to date of delivery of Maine granite for
use in U.S.Mint building, and I have the honor to advise you that the
sub-contractors for same inform the material will be ready for shipment within sixty days from this date,and will thereafter follow promptly.

          Very respectfully,

              J.A.McIntyre

                  T.

Denver,Colo.August 13th,1900.

Lee Ollery,Esq.,

      Superintendent of Construction,

          U.S.Mint (New),

Sir:-

      I have the honor to enclose for your acceptance the guaran
tee of the Celadon Terra Cotta Company as to color and quality of the
finials called for in your letter of late date. Trusting that this
will be satisfactory and meet the approval of the Supervising Architect, I am

              Very respectfully,

                  J.A.McIntyre

                    T.

Headquarters Department of the Colorado,

OFFICE OF THE CHIEF QUARTERMASTER.

Denver, Colorado, August 13,1900.

Superintendent of Construction,

U.S.Mint Building,

Denver,Colorado.

Dear Sir:

There has arrived at the Burlington Freight Depot,this city, one case stationery-140 lbs.for you,consigned to the care of this office on Government bill of lading 263,Washington to Denver,Aug.1, 1900. Please advise this office at your early convenience where you wish this box delivered,and oblige,

Yours Truly,

Major and Quartermaster,U.S.A.,
Chief Quartermaster.

4 5

TREASURY DEPARTMENT

OFFICE OF THE SUPERVISING ARCHITECT

Washington, **Aug. 15, 1900.**

The Superintendent of Construction,
United States (New) Mint,
Denver, Colorado.

Sir:

In reply to your letter of August 9th, requesting information regarding the construction of certain portions of terra-cotta partitions in the first story of the building under your charge, I have to say that as shown by drawings of present contract this work will not fit interior finish, therefore, this Office will entertain a proposition from the contractor to build a 6 inch terra-cotta wall from the 12 inch "I", to the ceiling between columns 22 and 27 omitting the unsupported terra-cotta and the additional thickness, and also omitting the terra-cotta over opening between columns 21 and 28, and as an offset to this omission to remove the two 12 inch channels between columns 21 and 28: This to be done without extra charge to the Government.

Such structural work as is necessitated by the interior finish will be provided for in the interior finish contract.

Respectfully,

Supervising Architect.

form 33.
Ed. 12-29-'94 —2,000.

46

Treasury Department,

OFFICE OF THE SUPERVISING ARCHITECT.

Washington, D. C., **August 15, 1900.**

Mr. **Lee Ullery,**

Supt. U. S. **Mint Building,**

Sir: **Denver, Colorado.**

I have to acknowledge the receipt of your *"Estimate of Funds"* required for the work on the building under your superintendence during **August, 1900,** , and to advise you that, as it appears the remittance of funds heretofore made to the Disbursing Agent on account of the appropriation for the building is sufficient to meet all vouchers issued or to be issued for expenditures on account of the work on the building, to and including the last day of the current month, no further remittance will be made to him at present.

Respectfully, yours,

Chief Executive Officer.

F.D.

DENVER. MINT (new).

D.

ENCLOSE.

TREASURY DEPARTMENT
OFFICE OF THE SUPERVISING ARCHITECT

Washington, August 18, 1900.

The Superintendent of Construction,

U. S. Mint (new),

Denver, Col.

Sir:

Your letter of the 14th instant is received, enclosing communication addressed to you the preceding day by Mr. J. A. McIntyre,
contractor for the erection of the building in your charge, in relation to shipment of Maine granite and substitution of same for
stone provided for in the contract with him.

Enclosed find copy of Department letter of this day addressed
to the contractor named, and you are now requested to make record
thereof, in order that the information may be available when com-
plying with Section 40 of printed "Instructions to Superintendents,"
in connection with final settlement, as related to the infliction
of the penalty.

Respectfully,

Supervising Architect.

TREASURY DEPARTMENT

OFFICE OF THE SECRETARY

Washington, **August 18, 1900.**

Mr. John A. McIntyre,

    Room 402 Cooper Building,

        Denver, Col.

Sir:

    The Superintendent of Construction of the U. S. Mint (new), Denver, Col., in letter of the 14th instant forwarded to the Supervising Architect of this Department a letter addressed by you to him on the proceding day. The communication relates to the substitution and delivery of Maine granite in lieu of the stone being used in the building, as provided for in a contract with you for foundation, superstructure, roof-covering, etc., of the U. S. Mint (new), Denver, Col. The statement made by you is noted, that you have been informed by your sub-contractors that the material will be ready for shipment within sixteen (16) days from August 13th, and will thereafter follow promptly.

    Your attention is specially called to the second paragraph of Department letter of the 2nd instant, in which it is understood and agreed that such substitution must not affect the time for the completion of the work, etc., and, in view of the penalty clause forming part of the contract, it would seem that your interests would demand that the completion of the entire work as embraced in the contract must be accomplished without further delay, and it should be unnecessary for this Department to suggest to you that you take such steps as may be required, urging upon your sub-contractors the delivery of the material with all dispatch.

Copy of this letter has been forwarded to the Superintendent of Construction, in order that his records may be complete when the Department is giving consideration to the penalty clause at final settlement of the account with you.

Respectfully,

(Signed) F. N. Vanderlip

Assistant Secretary.

C. E. T
X K. T.

S.

V.

F. N. Franklin

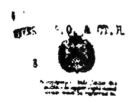

TREASURY DEPARTMENT
OFFICE OF THE SUPERVISING ARCHITECT

Washington, August 22, 190_.

Superintendent of Construction,

U. S. Mint (New),

Denver, Colorado.

Sir:-

You are advised that the Department has this day rejected the proposals for erection of partitions, etc., in the Weather Bureau Offices in the Post Office and Court House building at Denver, Colorado for the reason that the prices were considered excessive, and it being decided to change the character of the partitions from iron to terracotta.

You are hereby directed to prepare a new specification for this work, providing for terra-cotta partitions, and to then invite proposals for the performance of the work, forwarding all received through the Custodian of the building with your recommendations as to acceptance.

Respectfully,

_____

Acting Supervising Architect.

Re. New Mint.

TREASURY DEPARTMENT

OFFICE OF THE SUPERVISING ARCHITECT

Washington, August 25, 1900.

Superintendent of Construction,

U.S.Mint (New),

Denver, Colorado.

In view of the statements and recommendations contained in your letter of the 22nd instant, and the public exigency which requires the immediate performance of the work, you are hereby authorized to incur an expenditure not to exceed three dollars ($3.00) for repairs to plumbing in the temporary office used by you as Superintendent of Construction in connection with work at the building under your charge.

Upon satisfactory completion of the work certify and issue voucher in triplicate herewith, the Disbursing Agent having this day been directed to make payment thereof from funds in his hands on account of the "Appropriation for "U.S.Mint, Denver, Colorado".

Respectfully,

Acting Supervising Architect.

TREASURY DEPARTMENT

Office of the Supervising Architect

Washington.   August 26, 1900.

Superintendent of Construction,

U. S. Mint Bldg.,

Denver, Col.

Sir:

In order that your record may be complete, enclosed find copy of express letter of this day addressed to Mr. John A. McIntyre, contractor for the erection of the building under your charge. Reference is also made in Department letter addressed to him under date this date with respect in relation to date of the delivery of Metal Work.

Respectfully,

Acting Supervising Architect.

August 20, 1900.

Mr. John A. McIntyre,

Room 402 Cooper Building,

Denver, Colo.

Sir:

Through inadvertence, Department letter of the 18th instant referred to your having made the statement that Maine granite would be shipped within sixteen (16) days from August 18th, while the statement made by you was that the granite would be ready for shipment within sixty (60) days from August 18th, for use under a contract with you for the erection of the U. S. Mint (new), Denver, Colorado.

Respectfully,

Assistant Secretary.

U.S. Mint (mail)
Denver, Colo

This is to request you to remove the obstructions which have been placed upon the lots belonging to the estate of John ..., and facing ... and the 10th Street ... alley running east & west ...

MARGARET ... NS, Administratrix

AGENT

U.S. MINT (new).

TREASURY DEPARTMENT
OFFICE OF THE SUPERVISING ARCHITECT

Washington, September 7,1900.

To Superintendent of Construction,

U. S. Mint (new),

Denver, Col.

Sir:

Receipt of your letter of the 29th ultimo is hereby acknowledged, relative to the non-receipt of sample of granite approved for the star member of the cornice of the building under your charge.

Through some mistake the sample was not forwarded to you, but it will now sent to you this day under separate cover.

Respectfully,

Supervising Architect.

Denver Colo. Sept.11 1900.

Leo Ullery Esq.
  Supt. Construction
    New Mint. Denver Colo.
  Dear Sir.

Referring to the use of " iron cramps" in the copings on the areas and coal vault walls of the U. S. Mint Building under your charge, I have to suggest that I be allowed to use crystalized trap rock dowels similar to sample herewith submitted to you, for the iron cramps called for in plans and specifications. I make this request as I am convinced that the useof stone dowels will prove more satisfactory than the iron cramps. I will furnish and put in place at each vertical joint in said copings

acrystalized trap rock dowel, as per sample, $1\frac{1}{4}" \times 2" \times 2"$ and anchor the cop—

ing at corners of area and coal vault walls to the brick work beneath with

a similar dowel let $1\frac{1}{2}"$ into the bottom bed of the coping and $2\frac{1}{2}"$ into

brickwork, for the sum of Twenty($20.) Dollars which amount is intended

solely to cover the extra cost of labor in setting the dowelled stones.

I would also request permission to substitute without charge to the

Government, similar dowels to those specified above for the slate dowels

called for in the steps and buttresses.

Very Respectfully,

(Signed) J. A. McIntyre.
T.

Form No. 168.

THE WESTERN UNION TELEGRAPH COMPANY.

·INCORPORATED·

21,000 OFFICES IN AMERICA. CABLE SERVICE TO ALL THE WORLD.

This Company TRANSMITS and DELIVERS messages only on conditions limiting its liability, which have been assented to by the sender of the following message.
Errors can be guarded against only by repeating a message back to the sending station for comparison, and the Company will not hold itself liable for errors or delays
in transmission or delivery of Unrepeated Messages, beyond the amount of tolls paid thereon, nor in any case where the claim is not presented in writing within sixty days
after the message is filed with the Company for transmission.
This is an UNREPEATED MESSAGE, and is delivered by request of the sender, under the conditions named above. 365

THOS. T. ECKERT, President and General Manager.

RECEIVED at 1114 to 1118 17th St., Denver, Colo.   NEVER CLOSED.

52 CH CT NR. 30 Paid Govt.

Washington, DC Sep 12-900

Supt of Construction

U S Mint,Bldg. New. DENVER,COL.

In view of your recommendation you

are authorized to accept piece egg

and Dart delivered

J K Taylor,

Supervising Architect.

9:30 a.m.

DENVER MINT.

ENCLOSURE

TREASURY DEPARTMENT

OFFICE OF THE SUPERVISING ARCHITECT

Washington, Sept. 17,1900.

The Superintendent of Construction,

New Mint Building,

Denver, Colorado.

Sir:-

I enclose herewith, for your information and the files of
your office, copy of a letter of even date accepting the proposal
of Mr. J. A. McIntyre for making modifications and omission of terra cotta and steel work between columns 22 and 27 and 21 and 28, in
the first story of the building in your charge, without additional
expense to the Government, which letter explains itself.

Respectfully,

Supervising Architect.

J.G.

DENVER MINT.

Sept.17,1900.

Mr. J. A. McIntyre,
402 Cooper Building,
Denver, Colorado,

Sir:-

In view of the statement and recommendation contained in letter of the 23rd ultimo from the Superintendent of Construction of the New Mint Building at Denver, Colorado, your proposal of the 22nd ultimo, addressed to him, to substitute 4" for 13" terra cotta partitions between columns 36 and 37, and remove channels between columns 31 and 36, and omit terra cotta partitions from said channels to ceiling, fireproofing soffits as elsewhere, and to do all work in connection therewith, at the above named building, as directed by the Superintendent, without additional expense to the Government, is hereby accepted, a public exigency requiring the said changes to be made.

It is understood and agreed that these changes are not to affect the time for the completion of the entire work as fixed in your original contract; that the same are without prejudice to any and all rights of the United States thereunder; and are without prejudice, also, to the rights of the United States against the sureties on the bond executed for the faithful fulfillment of the contract.

Please promptly acknowledge the receipt of this letter, a copy of which has been forwarded to the Superintendent.

Respectfully,

Acting Secretary.

B.
O.V.B.

DENVER, COLO., MINT BLDG.

Form 34.
Ed. 13 10 97 2,000. }

ADVISING OF REMITTANCE OF FUNDS.

Treasury Department,

OFFICE OF SUPERVISING ARCHITECT,

Washington, D. C., September 20, 190089 .

Sir:

Your estimate of funds required during the month of September, 1900,

xxxsxxfor the work under your charge, is received. I have to advise you that a

remittance of $ 20,000.00, xxto James L. Rodges,

Disbursing Agent, has been requested.

Respectfully yours,

Chief Executive Officer.

Mr. Lee Ullery,

Superintendent U. S. Mint Building,

Denver, Colorado.

F.D.

AUTHORITY FOR OPEN-MARKET PURCHASE.

(All letters in reply to official communications must refer to initial in upper right-hand corner.)

Treasury Department,

OFFICE OF THE SUPERVISING ARCHITECT,

Washington, D. C., September 20, 1900.

erintendent of Construction,

   U.S. Mint Building, (new),

     Denver, Colorado.

Sir:

     In view of the request and recommendation contained in your letter of the 14th instant and the public exigency requiring the immediate delivery of the articles and performance of the work you are hereby authorized to incur an expenditure not exceeding five dollars ($5.00)

in securing in open market at lowest prevailing rates:

photographic views of work on the building $ 5.00

     Your attention is called to printed "Instructions to Superintendents," and you will issue and certify vouchers on account of the above in accordance therewith, payment to be made from the appropriation for "U.S. Mint Building, Denver, Colo."

       Respectfully yours,

                Chief Executive Officer.

Superintendent of Construction,

U. S. Mint (new),

Denver (Col)

Mr. ___ ___ _____, the Custodian of the ___ ___ Post Office building at Pueblo, Col., has reported the completion of repairs ___ ___ heating apparatus at the building in his custody.

The nature of the performance of the work here _____ ___ may ___ ___ ___ information in regard thereto before ___ ___ files of the ___ ___

In regard to repairs of heating apparatus, you are informed that Mr. ___ ___, Inspector of Heating, Hoisting and Ventilation ___ is now under instructions to visit the building and make examination of such work.

You are now directed to proceed to the building ___ ___ as an expert on the ___ repairs of ___ of heating and ___ ___ of the work.

Upon completion of this duty return to Denver, Col., and submit the Supervising Architect of this Department a report embodying results of the examination, with such suggestions and recommendations as may seem to you to be in line with the best interests of the

- -

Government.

Your actual traveling and subsistence expenses while in the performance of this duty will be paid from appropriations under the control of the Supervising Architect.

Respectfully,

H A Taylor

Assistant Secretary.

S.

T.

TREASURY DEPARTMENT

OFFICE OF THE SUPERVISING ARCHITECT

WASHINGTON

The Superintendent of Construction,

Sir:

DENVER MINT (NEW).

September 19,1908.

Mr. John A.McIntyre,
        Cooper Building,
            Denver, Colorado.

Sir;

In view of the statements contained in letter of the 18th instant from the superintendent of construction of the New Mint Building at Denver, Colorado, your proposal, dated the 11th instant, addressed to him, in amount twenty dollars ($20.00) to substitute crystallized trap rock dowels, in accordance with sample submitted, in lieu of the iron cramps required by the drawings and specification forming a part of your contract for the superstructure,etc., of the said building,is hereby accepted, the same being deemed reasonable, this to be considered as an addition to your contract, and a public exigency requiring a change in the work.

You will be also permitted to substitute similar dowels to those above specified for the slate dowels called for in the steps and buttresses, without additional cost to the Government.

It is understood and agreed that this change is not to affect the time for the completion of the work as required by the terms of your contract; that the same is without prejudice to any and all rights of the United States thereunder; and without prejudice, also, to any and all rights of the United States against the sureties on the bond executed for the faithful fulfillment of the con.....

J.A.McIntyre.   Page 2.

    Please promptly acknowledge the receipt of this letter,
a copy of which has been forwarded to the superintendent of
the building, for his information and guidance.

                    Respectfully,

S.   Assistant Secretary.
G.W.D.

M.T.R.

Sept. 20th, 1905.

To Stlery Esq.,

Supt. of Construction, U. S. Sine Dept.

Denver, Colorado.

Sir:

I am in receipt of a letter from the Department of Justice enclosing bond, contract and specifications for construction of the post office building at Pueblo, directing that suit be brought for the recovery of damages for defective workmanship, ... al be used in the construction of the same, It appears from the employees to me that you made certain investigations of the building after the ... completion of the work.

I tried to ... personally and called at the time into ..., and I will therefore take the liberty of requesting you to call at my office at your earliest convenience or to indicate a time when it will be convenient for you to come to my office. I am desirous of seeing a copy of the printed document ... the ... improvements." a copy of which I presume you have.

Respectfully,

U. S. Attorney.

... by Hgy

Mr. Lee Ullery,

Superintendent of Construction,

Mint Building, Denver, Colorado,

Sir:-

I enclose herewith Disbursing Clerk Thomas J. Hobbs'
check, No. 179033, drawn to your order, in the sum of.......$14.70,
for expenses incurred by you in travelling from Denver to Pueblo,
Colorado, and return, under orders from this Department.

Please acknowledge receipt.

Respectfully,

Acting Chief Executive Officer.

Inclosure.

TREASURY DEPARTMENT

Office of the Supervising Architect.

Washington,

October 8, 1900.

Superintendent of Construction.

U. S. Mint (New),

Denver, Colo.

Sir:

Your letter of the 29th ultimo is received suggesting method of testing terra cotta floor arches at the building under your charge.

The statements made by you are noted, and it has been determined to apply the necessary tests, but in a manner somewhat varying from that suggested by you. The specification forming part of a contract with Mr. J. A. McIntyre for the erection of the building, on page D, provides for the testing of the terra cotta arches, which test is to be made at the expense of the contractor. The standard required is that the arches must be capable of sustaining 600 lbs. per square foot. The Government can select such method as may seem to it best, by testing any area of any span, provided that no square foot shall be required to withstand a weight greater than 600 lbs.

Inclosed find miscellaneous drawing No. 20 indicating the manner in which the arches must be tested, which will include an area not less than 10 square feet, extending across the entire span of arch in width between two and three feet.

The contractor, as governed by the specification, must be responsible for all damage resulting from tests, and in view of this, this office is prepared to give consideration to any other scheme which might be submitted, provided that the formula and test of arch, or portion of arch, shall correspond to one now suggested.

You are requested, therefore, to give the matter further consideration, and to resubmit the matter to this office with such suggestions as may be proper. It must be understood that the tests must be frequent under the circumstances, in order that as little floor as possible may have to be finally rejected, especially where partitions are located. In the event that defects develop as a result of the test, the defective work must be removed and new work substituted therefor, as fully provided for in the specification.

By reason of the length of time since the floor arches were laid and the seasons through which they have been exposed, special care must be exercised in regard to this matter, and if the tests do not eliminate all suspected arches, you must report for further instructions.

Respectfully,

(Supervising Architect.

the substitution requested, I can avoid all danger to both bed and line of the cornice by avoiding any strain thereon and at the same time secure more rapid advancement of the work.

Very Respectfully,
(signed) J. A. McEntyre
J.

TREASURY DEPARTMENT

OFFICE OF THE SUPERVISING ARCHITECT

Washington,   October 5, 1900

Superintendent of Construction,

   U. S. Mint (New),

      Denver, Colorado.

         (Office of the Supervising Architect.)

Sir.

       Your communication of the 26th ultimo addressed to the Chief of
the Division of Appointments of this Department, has been referred to
this office for recommendation, in relation to the leave of absence
granted Mr. Herbert K. Quigley, Inspector in connection with work on
building under your charge.

       Your statements are noted and your attention is called to my
sent telegram this day requesting your presence in this city and a
to office telegram directing you to arrange for Mr. Quigley's presence
at the building during your absence, and you are now advised that
upon return to your duties at Denver, you will again bring this matter
to the attention of the office, when consideration will be given to
granting Mr. Quigley any leave which may be due him and to allowing him
for any days already granted but not used by him on account of his
necessary presence at the building.

                     Respectfully,

                                    [signature]
                                    Supervising Architect.

Lee Ullery Esq.

Supt Construction.

U. S. Mint (new)

Sir.

I have the honor to acknowledge receipt of your letter
October 9th. 1900 relative to substitution of expansion, for
anchor bolts for roof beams in top member of cornice.

Very respectfully.

J. A. McIntyre

TREASURY DEPARTMENT

OFFICE OF THE SUPERVISING ARCHITECT

*In replying to this Letter the
initials in upper right-hand
corner must be referred to.*

Washington, **October 9, 1900.**

The Superintendent of Construction,

    United States (new) Mint,

        Denver, Colorado.

Sir:

    I am in receipt of your letter of the 3rd instant
relative to the use of wheel guards for the approaches
to the building under your charge, and in reply I have to
advise you that this will be taken care of in the drawings for the interior finish.

              Respectfully,

                    Supervising Architect.

R.

Division of Construction,
Mint Building,

Denver, Colorado.

. . .

. . With interest . . .

. . . .

. . . . duly authorized to incur

. . dollars and fifty cents . .

. . . .

DENVER, COLORADO NEW MINT.

TREASURY DEPARTMENT

OFFICE OF THE SUPERVISING ARCHITECT

Washington, October 16, 18

The Superintendent of Construction,

United States (new) Mint,

Denver, Colorado.

Sir:

I am in receipt of your letter of the 8th instant with enclosure from the contractor relative to the substitution of "Expansion" for the Anchor bolts required in connection with the roof rafters of the building under your charge, and in reply I have to advise you that no change will be permitted from the Anchor bolts shown on the drawings.

The difficulty in fitting the rafters can be easily overcome by making slightly oblong holes therein for the anchors.

Respectfully,

Architect.

TREASURY DEPARTMENT

OFFICE OF THE SECRETARY

114

Washington, **October 20, 1900.**

Mr. Lee Ullery,

    Superintendent of Construction of Public Buildings,

        U. S. Mint, Denver, Colorado.

Sir:

    I have to inform you that Mr. Eugene C. Wilson has this day
been reinstated and appointed a Watchman in connection with the
building under your superintendency, with compensation at the rate
of $840 per annum, to commence from assignment to duty and sub-
scribing to oath of office.

    You are authorized to issue and certify vouchers for his ser-
vices accordingly.

    The services of this Watchman are to be used solely in the
interests of the Government, and not in any manner for the protection of the contractor's materials.

                Respectfully,

                       Secretary.

T.

DENVER MINT.

In replying to this Letter the initials in upper right-hand corner must be referred to.

TREASURY DEPARTMENT

OFFICE OF THE SUPERVISING ARCHITECT

Washington,   Oct. 27, 1900.

The Superintendent of Construction,

    New Mint Building,

        Denver, Colorado.

Sir:-

    The following telegram was this day sent to Mr. J. A. Mc-
Intyre, contractor for the superstructure, etc., of the building
in your charge:

        "Use stones now cut six feet, instead of six feet
six, for cornice, Denver Mint".

    You will please be governed in accordance with the above
in passing upon the work.

        Respectfully,

                    (Supervising Architect.

J.G.

DENVER. MINT (NEW).

MGD

*In replying to this Letter the
initials in upper right-hand
corner must be referred to.*

TREASURY DEPARTMENT

OFFICE OF THE SUPERVISING ARCHITECT

Washington, October 22, 1900.

The Superintendent of Construction,

    U. S. Mint (new),

        Denver, Colorado.

Sir:

    Referring to Department letter of the 20th instant, notifying you of the reinstatement and appointment of Mr. Eugene C. Wilson as watchman at the building under your charge, you are informed that the watchman named was, by wire, assigned to duty on the 20th instant, to commence on and include the 22nd instant, conditioned upon his subscribing to oath of office on that day.

        Respectfully,

                                  Supervising Architect.

DENVER,COLO.,MINT BUILDING.

Form 22.
S4.12-25-74-2,000.}

Treasury Department,

OFFICE OF THE SUPERVISING ARCHITECT.

Washington, D. C.,   October 25, 1900.

Mr. Lee Ullery,

Supt. U. S. Mint Building,

Denver, Colorado.

Sir :

I have to acknowledge the receipt of your "Estimate of Funds" required for the work on the building under your superintendence during October, 1900,   , and to advise you that, as it appears the remittance of funds heretofore made to the Disbursing Agent on account of the appropriation for the building is sufficient to meet all vouchers issued or to be issued for expenditures on account of the work on the building, to and including the last day of the current month, no further remittance will be made to him at present.

Respectfully, yours,

Acting   Chief Executive Officer.

F.D.

The Suffin Clay Mfg. Co.

Mr. Grinnell's.

Please say that the [illegible]
you to acknowledge receipt of this [illegible]
say that the supervising architects
has been informed concerning the
[illegible] mentioned in the [illegible]

Yours [illegible]
Su[illegible]

FOSTER, ..., MINT ....

TREASURY DEPARTMENT

OFFICE OF THE SUPERVISING ARCHITECT

Washington   October 24, 190...

The Superintendent of Construction,
    New Mint Building,
        Denver, Colorado.
    Care, Supervising Architect, Washington D. C.

Sir:

I have to acknowledge receipt of your letter of the 24th
instant, in which you indicate that it is possible that J. A.
McIntyre, contractor for the foundations, superstructure, etc.,
of the building under your charge, may apply for permission to
make a change in the manufacture and character of the terra
cotta floor arches which have already been approved and that
the terra cotta arches which have been delivered are not being
properly stored and covered.

You are informed that this office will not reconsider the
approval already made or authorize a change, unless the contractor states good and sufficient reasons therefor, showing
that the Government's interests will be best served by making
the said change, and you are hereby instructed to inform the
contractor that should any material be damaged on account of
exposure to the elements, the same will be rejected.

Respectfully,

J. K. Taylor

Supervising Architect.

W. T. M.

TREASURY DEPARTMENT
OFFICE OF THE SECRETARY
Washington, November 1, 19..

Superintendent of Construction,
Mint (New), Denver, Colorado.
(Care of Supervising Architect.)

Sir: Referring to Department telegram of the 6th ultimo ordering you to the office of the Supervising Architect of this Department with a view to proceed to work at the building under your charge you are directed to return to Denver and resume your duties at once.

Your actual traveling and subsistence expenses incident to the above will be paid from appropriations under the control of the Supervising Architect.

Respectfully,

Assistant Secretary.

TREASURY DEPARTMENT
OFFICE OF THE SUPERVISING ARCHITECT

Washington, November 19, 1910.

The Superintendent of Construction,

New Mint Building,

Denver, Colo.

Sir:

In preparing the plans for the heating and ventilating apparatus for the building under your charge, it is found that a discrepancy exists between the intended and actual location of the foul air flue outlets. There is forwarded herewith under separate cover drawing No. 6-A/Ha, and you are instructed to obtain from the contractor a proposal for the changes shown thereon, i.e., modifications of the galvanised iron flue linings, provision of openings in walls and floors, and furnishing and placing of new 9" beams for support of future partition walls; and to forward such proposal to this office with your definite recommendations.

Respectfully,

J. K. Bagley
Acting Supervising Architect.

M.M.

(PRINTED HEADING).

Denver,Colo.Nov.21,1900.

Lee Ullery,Esq.,

Supt.Construction, U.S.Mint (New),

Denver, Colorado.

Sir:-

Replying to your letter Nov.20th instant,requesting proposition for change in method of "pointing",using crushed granite therein, I have the honor to say I will make said change using equal parts Red Diamond cement and crushed Arkins granite for the sum of $350.00.

Very Respectfully,

(Signed) J.A.McIntyre.
T.

(PRINTED HEADING).

Denver,Colo.,Nov.23rd,1900.

Lee Ullery,Esq.,

      Supt.Construction, Denver, Colorado.

Sir:-

      Replying to your letter 22nd instant I have the honor
to say, I will omit coloring matter and special treatment from
mortar used for "pointing" out United States Mint Building,under
my contract, without additional expense to the United States.

      Very respectfully,

        (Signed) J.A.McIntyre.

            T.

Denver,Colo.,November 24,1900

Mr.Lee Ullery,

    Superintendent of Construction,

        U.S.Mint Building, City.

Sir:-

      In answer to yours of the 21st instant,in which you say you cannot understand my letter of the 21st instant, permit me to again answer yours of the 19th.

      We have in our city,two systems of sewerage -- storm and sanitary.

      Our storm sewer is intended to carry off rain water only, but we have no objections to connecting cellar drains or wagon wash to same,but we do not allow any house fixtures to connect with storm sewer,either directly or indirectly,such as basins,sinks,bath tubs, closets and all house fixtures must be connected with sanitary sewer.

      All sinks which are used in living apartments,such as kitchens or pantry sinks must be provided with a grease trap.

      Allow me to call your attention to the fact that we have a creek running through the center of our city which is dry seven months in the year.

      Our storm sewer empties into this creek at the most convenient place while our sanitary sewer is conducted to lower end of city.

      Small quantities of water such as you might discharge through sinks and basins,if discharged into storm sewer,would remain on surface of creek bottom,become foul and stagnant and under no consideration would this be allowed from a sanitary point of view.

      Let me again call your attention to the fact that all house fixtures must connect with sanitary sewer.

      The storm sewer is intended to carry off rain water only.

         Respectfully yours,

            (Signed) H.F.McBryde
            Plumbing Inspector.

Form 32.
Ed.12-29-'94—2,000. }

Treasury Department,

OFFICE OF THE SUPERVISING ARCHITECT,

Washington, D. C.,   November 21, 1900.

.Mr. Lee Ullery,

    Supt. U. S. Mint Building,

        Denver, Colorado.

Sir:

    I have to acknowledge the receipt of your "Estimate of Funds" required for the work on the building under your superintendence during **November,**

    1900,   XXXX , *and to advise you that, as it appears the remittance of funds heretofore made to the Disbursing Agent on account of the appropriation for the building is sufficient to meet all vouchers issued or to be issued for expenditures on account of the work on the building, to and including the last day of the current month, no further remittance will be made to him at present.*

        Respectfully, yours,

                      Acting   *Chief Executive Officer.*

F.D.

Enclosure.

TREASURY DEPARTMENT

Office of the Supervising Architect

Washington, November 24, 1900.

Mr. Lee Ullery,

Superintendent of Construction,

Mint Building, Denver, Colorado.

Sir:-

I return herewith, approved upon its face, voucher, in duplicate, drawn in your favor, in the sum of.........$179.50, for expenses incurred by you in traveling under orders from this Department, for presentation to the Disbursing Agent of the building in your charge, for payment from funds in his hands appropriated for "Mint Building, Denver, Colorado," as per instructions this day given.

Respectfully,

Acting Chief Executive Officer.

Washington   November 24, 1906.

of Construction,
lding,
ver, Colorado.

. . . .
. . . 10th instant, and the public exigency requiring the
. . . . of the articles and performance of the work you
. . . authorized to incur an expenditure not exceeding six dol-
. . seventy-five cents ($6.75)
. . . . market at lowest prevailing rates

. . rent for six months from the 1st instant. $4.75

November 27, 1905.

Mr. Ernest L. Thomson,
803 Ernest & Cranmer Block,
Denver, Colo.

Sir:

This Department is in receipt of your communication of the 18th instant, in which you request that Mr. Lew Wiley, the Superintendent of Construction of the new Mint building at Denver, Colo., be permitted to appear and testify as a witness in the case of the United States for the use and benefit of George P. Schumacher v. John A. McIntyre and The United States Fidelity & Guaranty Company.

In reply you are advised that no objection will be interposed to Mr. Wiley's appearing as a witness in said case, provided he is regularly subpoenaed for that purpose, and Mr. Wiley will be so advised.

Respectfully,

The Superintendent of Construction.

United States (Bra) Mint,

Denver, Colorado.

Sir:

In reply to your telegram of the 24th instant,
I yesterday wired as follows:

"Telegram your plumbing for telegram
are received if before deciding."

It is not customary to follow the requirements
of the City regulations regarding plumbing, as to date
have furnished subject to the approval of the City
Inspector; the City of Denver Government having no
jurisdiction whatever over the site upon which the
building will soon unless so empowered. It may however
from time to time that objection is necessary due to
the Government methods, in the event of believing your
mission to self constructed to the great expense, we
have the City's views and if it the plumbing are
followed, but if ....
given you to proceed with the new......
ing conferred with these officials, stating plainly the
facts in the case. See Department telegram of this date.

erintendent of Construction.

  U. S. Mint Building,

     Denver, Colorado.

     In view of the request and the memorandum of verbal

order of the 23rd ultimo, and the public exigency re-

mediate delivery of the articles and performance of

action in incurring an expenditure of five dollars

hereby approved,

    in emecting in open market at lowest prevailing rates

photographic views of work on the building

DENVER MINT (new)

TREASURY DEPARTMENT

OFFICE OF THE SUPERVISING ARCHITECT

Washington,   Dec.1,1900.

Superintendent of Construction,
　　New Mint Building,
　　　　Denver, Colorado.

Sir:-

　　　　I have to acknowledge the receipt of your letter of the
22d ultimo, containing a proposal of John A.McIntyre,the contractor for the superstructure of the building in your charge,
in amount $1,500.00, for making certain changes in the work
included therein,and you are directed to reject the said proposal,as it is unreasonable and excessive.

　　　　Please obtain from the contractor a proposal for omitting
three granite steps in basement; omitting 8" terra cotta partition in basement near column #18,and for omitting such portion
of the brick chimney as is included in his contract but not
yet completed.

　　　　Upon receipt of the proposal you will forward it to this
office with your definite recommendation.

　　　　　　Respectfully,

　　　　　　　　Acting Supervising Architect.

J.S.S.

COPY.   / '

Printed Heading.

Denver Colo. Dec. 3 1900.

Lee Ullery Esq.

      Supt. Construction.

         Denver Colorado.

Sir.

    Replying to your letter Dec. 3rd. relating to certain changes in struc
tion of U. S. Mint Building under your cherge. I have the honor to say . I
have carefully gone over the plans and am prepared to carry out the changes
as shown on Drawing 5-1/2 and your letter November 22 ultimo. for the sum
of five hundred dollars.

          Very respectfully,

             (Signed) --J. A. McIntyre.
                        T

DENVER, COLO. MINT (NEW).

TREASURY DEPARTMENT

OFFICE OF THE SUPERVISING ARCHITECT

Washington, December 3, 1900.

99.

The Superintendent of Construction,

    Mint Building,

        Denver, Colo.

Sir:

    I have to acknowledge receipt of your letter of the 23rd ultimo containing proposals for changing the pointing of the granite in the building under your charge.

    You are directed to reject the same on account of being excessive, and you are requested to obtain from the contractor a proposal for pointing all stone work with neat cement in lieu of that mixed with sand, coloring and special mixtures required by the specification, and forward it to this office as soon as possible with your definite recommendations.

          Respectfully,

Supervising Architect.

H.M.

TREASURY DEPARTMENT

OFFICE OF THE SUPERVISING ARCHITECT

Washington, December 4, 1900.

The Superintendent of Construction,

   U.S.Mint (New),

     Denver, Colorado.

Sir:

   Your letter of the 22nd ultimo is received, mainly in relation to principal member of main cornice in the building under your charge, to be supplied under a contract with J.A.McIntyre, and you are informed, as far as relates to cutting of the member, that same should be accepted if the cutting conforms to that shown on sample forwarded to you August 2nd last.

   In regard to lack of sharpness in fillets and arrises, you are informed that they must be finished sharp and clean, in true accord with proper workmanlike results.

   In regard to patches, you must reject all patched stone-work, as being at variance with the terms of the agreement.

   Please advise this office further in regard to the matter.

     Respectfully,

          Supervising Architect.

W.C.R.

(PRINTED HEADING).

Denver,Colorado, Dec.7,1900.

Lee Ullery,Esq.,

Superintendent of Construction,

Denver, Colorado.

Sir :-

Replying to your letter Dec.6th inst., asking for proposal to substitute neat cement for cement and sand,in pointing the
United States Mint Building, this city, I have the honor to say.

I will substitute neat Red Diamond Cement for said pointing,for the sum of Twenty Dollars,which said sum is the exact cost
of the additional cement,less the sand omitted.

Very respectfully,

(Signed) J.A.McIntyre,

T.

(PRINTED HEADING).

Denver,Colo.,December 11,1900.

Lee Ullery,
                Superintendent of Construction,
                        Denver, Colorado.

Sir:-

Replying to your favor December 8th, I have the honor to say,while fully appreciating the facts set forth therein,yet the statements made in my letter of 7th instant are still facts,i.e. the terra cotta has been manufactured,and I will be compelled to pay for same. The stone has been quarried and I have been requested to make payment for same. I cannot therefore retire from the position taken in my letter of 7th instant supra, and should the Supervising Architect see fit to make any deduction from my contract price for said work, I shall for the present be compelled to submit,but, I shall ask that I be advised of the exact amount of such deduction,and the basis on which same are fixed.

Very respectfully,

(Signed) J.A.McIntyre.

(PRINTED HEADING).

Denver, Colo., Dec.7,1900.

Lee Ullery, Esq.,

      Superintendent of Construction,

        Denver, Colorado.

Sir:-

    Replying to your letter, Dec.4 instant, regarding omissions from contract for U.S.Mint building, I have the honor to say.

    I cannot see my way clear to deductions on account of 8" T.C. partition near column 18, as the sub-contractor for this work will object to any deduction, they having manufactured all the material, stored same, and shipped a greater part thereof. Regarding the three granite steps in basement, much the same condition exists, the stone having been quarried and shipped and some work done thereon.

    I cannot in view of the above make any proposition looking to a deduction from my contract price on account of said omissions.

        Very respectfully,

           (Signed) J.A.McIntyre,
                    T.

DENVER MINT (new)

Enclosure.

In replying to this Letter the initials in upper right-hand corner must be referred to.

TREASURY DEPARTMENT

OFFICE OF THE SUPERVISING ARCHITECT

Washington, Dec.13,1900

Superintendent of Construction,
        New Mint Building,
            Denver, Colorado.

Sir :-

I enclose herewith, for your information and the files
of your office, a copy of Department letter of even date, accepting the proposal of J.A.McIntyre, the contractor for the
superstructure, etc. of the building in your charge, in amount
twenty dollars ($20.00), to substitute a mortar of neat Red
Diamond Portland cement, in lieu of cement and sand, for pointing the joints of the granite work, all as stated in detail
in the said letter of acceptance.

You are hereby authorized to certify and issue vouchers
on account of the work, as required by the terms of the contract and the printed "Instructions to Superintendents," payment of which vouchers the Disbursing Agent has been authorized to make from the appropriation for Mint Building, Denver,
Colorado.

                        Respectfully,

                        James Know

                        (Acting Supervising Architect.

J.S.S.

Dec.15,1900.

Mr. J.A.McIntyre,
    Cooper Building,
        Denver,Colorado.

Sir:-

In view of the statement and recommendation contained
in letter of the 8th instant from the superintendent of construction of the new Mint Building at Denver,Colorado, your
proposal, dated the 7th instant, addressed to him, in amount
twenty dollars ($20.00),is hereby accepted to substitute a
mortar of neat Red Diamond Portland cement for pointing the
joints of the granite work, in lieu of cement and sand, with
coloring matter and mixture to render the mortar impervious
to moisture, the same being deemed reasonable and a public
exigency requiring this substitution,which is to be considered
as an addition to your contract for the superstructure,etc
of the building, for which your original proposal was accepted March 29,1898.

It is understood and agreed that this addition is not
to affect the time for the completion of the work,as required
by the terms of your contract;that the same is without prejudice to any and all rights of the United States thereunder;and
without prejudice,also, to any and all rights of the United
States against the sureties on the bond executed for the faithful fulfillment of the contract.
    Please promptly acknowledge the receipt of this letter,a
copy of which will be forwarded to the Superintendent.
                Respectfully,

I enclose herewith for your information and files as your
office a copy of Department letter of even date accepting the proposal of Mr. John A. McIntyre—forwarded in your letter of December 5, 1900— the contractor for the foundation, superstructure
and roof covering of the building in your charge, in amount five
hundred dollars ($500) for changes in galvanized iron flue linings
&c., as shown on drawing #6a, all as stated in detail in said
letter of acceptance.

You are hereby authorized to certify and issue vouchers on
account of the work as required by the terms of the contract and
printed "Instructions to Superintendents," the payment of which
vouchers the Disbursing Agent has been authorized to make from
funds remitted to him on account of the appropriation for the
within building, Denver, Colo.

In this connection you are advised that your understanding,
as stated in your letter of the 5th instant, that there are to be
no floor openings in any of vents "B" of attic floor line   is
correct.

Respectfully,

(Acting Supervising Architect.

December 14, 1906.

W. John W. ....
    Cooper Building,
        Denver, Colo.

Sir:

In view of the statement and recommendation contained in letter of December 3, 1906 from the Superintendent of Construction of the new Mint Building at Denver, Colorado, and in accordance with the approval of this Department, your proposal, dated December 3, 1906, addressed to him, in amount five hundred dollars ($500), is hereby accepted to furnish all labor and materials required to make certain changes in the .... linings, &c., included in your contract, for the foundation, superstructure, and roof covering of the said building (for which your original proposal was accepted March 30, 1905) in strict accordance with drawing #... and the instructions of the Superintendent, the same being deemed reasonable, this to be considered an addition to your said contract, ... requiring the immediate performance of the work.

It is understood and agreed that this addition is not to affect the time for the completion of the work as required by the terms of your contract; that the same is without prejudice to any and all rights of the United States thereunder; and without prejudice also to any and all rights of the United States against

.1

DENVER, COLO. NEW DIST MD'S.

the sureties of the bond executed for the faithful performance
of the contract.

Please promptly acknowledge the receipt of this letter
a copy of which will be forwarded the Superintendent for his information and guidance.

Respectfully,

Secretary.

V.

Treasury Department,

OFFICE OF THE SUPERVISING ARCHITECT,

Washington, D.   December 7, 1903.

Superintendent of Construction,

Mint Building, (new),

Denver, Colorado.

Sir:

view of the request and recommendations contained in your letter of the 3rd instant and the public exigency requiring the immediate delivery of the articles and performance of the work you **are hereby authorized to incur an expenditure not exceeding nine dollars ($9.00)**

in securing in open market at lowest prevailing rates

two tons of coal (2240 pounds each) for use
in Superintendent's office. $9.00

WESTERN UNION TELEGRAPH COMPANY.
———— INCORPORATED ————
D OFFICES IN AMERICA. CABLE SERVICE TO ALL THE WORLD.

D at 1114 to 1118 17th St., Denver, Colo.   **NEVER CLOSED.**

HT RY 11-26   22PAID..Gov't   710

ᴄton,D-C.?

Constru⬛⬛⬛⬛t,

Denver, Colo.

ave your reasons for telegram of twenty fifth before deci-

J. K. Taylor Supervising Archt.

Superintendent of Construction,
at States [illegible], Mint,

Denver, Colorado.

In reply to your letter of the 14th relative to the construction of certain in connection with the building under [illegible] in reply I have to state that th [illegible] for [illegible] are herein referred to be [illegible].

Respectfully,

[signature]

TREASURY DEPARTMENT

OFFICE OF THE SUPERVISING ARCHITECT

Washington, December 20, 7

The Superintendent of Construction,

United States New Mint,

Denver, Colorado.

Sir:

I have to advise you that Mr. Edwin B. Church, Superintendent of Machinery at the United States Mint, Philadelphia, Pennsylvania, has this day been directed to visit Denver, Colorado, for the purpose of obtaining full data regarding the machinery to be installed by the Mint Bureau in the building under your charge.

I have to request that you afford Mr. Church every facility possible for examining the building and studying the drawings in your possession.

Respectfully,

R.

TREASURY DEPARTMENT

OFFICE OF THE SUPERVISING ARCHITECT

Washington   December 22, 1900.

Superintendent of Construction,

　　U. S. Mint (New),

　　　　Denver, Colorado.

Sir:-

　　　　I have to acknowledge the receipt of your letters of
December 8th and 13th, together with sample of granite referred
to therein, all in connection with the material being furnished
for the upper course of cornice in the building under your charge.

　　　　The sub-contractor for this work has called at this office but as it is not permitted in any matters connected with
contracts to deal with other than the principal, it will be
necessary for the contractor of the building to fully comply
with the requirements of his contract relative to this stone,
subject to the accepted sample and wanting thereon.

　　　　　　Respectfully,

　　　　　　　　　　　　Supervising Architect.

to acknowledge the receipt of your letter of the

st, enclosing communication from the contractor

...mixture, etc. of the building in your charge,

...and make no deductions for certain omissions re-

...th office letter to you of the 1st instant, and you

are directed to require him to furnish all material

...rant, and where it is probable a change will be ma

...the material where it will be available for

h. You will also require the contractor to make

...effective repairs of the present columns, after

...ill not proceed with rebuilding until notified by

...u are directed to advise this office relative to

...of order required for the remainder of the ship

...or that the matter may be taken up at the time of

...tement with Mr.McIntyre

. . . .   December . . . .,

. . . .

$ 25,000   . .   James L. Hodges,

. . . .

. . . .

Acting . . . .

. . . Clerk,

. . . . . .   P.O.

Denver, Colo.

Superintendent of Construction,

    Mint Building (new),

      Denver, Colorado.

    the 24th instant

    you
are hereby authorized to incur an expenditure of five dollars
($5.00)

photographic views of work on the building. $5.00

TREASURY DEPARTMENT

OFFICE OF THE SUPERVISING ARCHITECT

Washington, January 8, 1901.

The Superintendent of Construction,

    United States (new) Mint,

      Denver, Colorado.

Sir:

    In reply to your inquiry of the 26th ultimo
I have to state that no changes, other than those
mentioned in your letter, are considered probable
in connection with the work on the building under
your charge.

        Respectfully,

                Supervising Architect.

R.

Treasury Department

January 1

Washington

Dee Ellery,

U.S.Mint,

Denver, Col.

MOD

DITE OR B.

The Super:

Sir:

D.t:

by Mr. J.

Please and

the Department of Welfare, and latter, both of the ... are in the New York Building, I have ... report as follows

The ... whether ... and workmanship, so far ... quoted, are in full accord with the requirements of the ...

In answer ... it may be stated in a general way ... a ... portions of the contract and ... have been ... on account of ... production but ... and ... work.

... in the ... specifications, page ... the "time will be ... work". And it undoubtedly ... the ... to the ... very ... work, I have ... ... made on ... "out."

... on the ... October ... sample of "the gas oil" work and ... field in said sample.

"As to whether the products delivered ... the ... ... reasonable ... the approved sample ... ... under ... above ... the ... the ... approved sample ... the ... sample ... ...

could that the quality of the sample ... It ... in view of the charges ... on ... ... for the purpose of determining whether the ... is reasonable herewith ... approved sample". I have ... quoted words from said Department letter ... reaching a conclusion ... that the ... and ... the sample for purpose of comparison. ... your inspector ... not warranted in doing so the terms of your letter of the 4th ...

My contention is that the cutting on the cornice stones is far inferior generally to the cutting shown on the poorest face of the approved sample, especially in this the ... are not cut sharp ... the arrises generally are not cut sharp ... I may state, however, that the finish of the ... on a number of the stone, approximates closely generally ... finish on the poorest face of the sample, although in spots it is left somewhat rough. In many stones the finish tool was not used sufficiently to produce an entire tooled surface, but left 'plucked' holes on the face of the cornice. There is no evidence of the finished faces of the ... portions of the stone that a ... was used, although it is well known that a rather smooth surface can be obtained by the pean hammer if the sur-face is gone over a sufficient number of times. In most of this work, however, and especially on the tooled members, the marks of the ... or pean hammer are ... far apart ... leaving quite a rough surface.

The ... portion of soffit of cornice between the edge of panels and the medallions is not tooled properly and should be brought up to the necessary finish. As noted before stated, the work now in place corresponds with the ... ap-out sample, and to put on a cornice which is only 58 feet from grade. The present rough finish would in my opinion, seriously mark the appearance of the building as com- ... its ... features. The profile of the cornice ... uniform, as I tested it with a ... template which I had made ... considerable trimming will be necessary after the stone is set to make the ... bed of the various members ... together at the joints. The profile ... likewise now corresponds ... the full size detail ... with your superintendent; it may however correspond with the model, which I understand was used, but the ... The ... the upper member of the ... the ... with ... beyond the face of the fillet immediately below ... a ... is shown by the full size detail ... it ... in the ... principal member. It ... section that there has ... length ... the stone, starting at a point ... feet ... being ... in a direction across ... face ... within 1¾" thereof, and apparently dies ... 1½" from the opposite side ... ... would make ... stone as the cornice ... its fillet immediately under ... ... for a distance of several inches ... middle of the stone the entire face ... stands ... at back slightly ... not ... ... the surface.

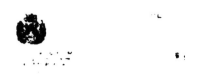

TREASURY DEPARTMENT

OFFICE OF THE SUPERVISING ARCHITECT

Washington, February 14, 1901

To Superintendent of Construction,

    U.S.Mint (New),

        Denver, Colorado.

Sir:

    Amplifying office telegram this day addressed to you in answer to your wire of the 13th instant, in relation to patching stone at the building under your charge, you are advised that the office interpretation of the report of Mr.I.W.Roberts, Superintendent, &c., of the 23rd ultimo, is that where patching is visible or where it is intended by the contractor to introduce supports below, which are not already in position, the stone involved is to be rejected; but, where the patching is not visible and where there were supports below at the date of Mr.Robert's visit, such stone may be accepted.

        Respectfully,

               Supervising Architect.

Denver, Colorado

hereby subscribe ... fifty ... ($0.50)

MINTER COLO. MINT BUILDING.

Treasury Department.

February 26, 1901.

Lee Ellery.

Mint Building,

Denver, Colorado.

the month of

February, 1901,

B.

Acting

Mr. Lee Ellery,

    Superintendent of Construction, U. S. Mint (New),

      Denver, Colo.

Sir:

    Your communication of the 18th instant, address-
ed to the Honorable Postmaster General, has been
referred to this office for its attention.

    You are informed that the action of the Post-
master at Denver in exacting registry fee upon official matter mailed by you, is proper and within
the Regulations.

    Under a recent decision of the Attorney Gen-
eral, official matter mailed elsewhere than at the
City of Washington, D. C., except upon official business of the Post Office Department, or relating to
the Census, or that presented by some officer of an
Executive Department, or Bureau thereof, who may be
temporarily absent from Washington upon official business pertaining to his office, is chargeable with
the usual registry fee.

Under this ruling, the matter in question is
not properly entitled to free registration.

Yours respectfully,

Edwin C Madden,,

Third Assistant Postmaster General.

Forwarded to Philadelphia Mint
by mistake.

A J Boyden
Supt Construction
New Phila Mint

To Superintendent of Construction,

    U. S. Mint Building (New),

        Denver, Colorado.

Sir:

　　You are requested to procure a sample of the water
furnished the building under your charge for use in connection
with the operation of the engineering plant thereof, and forward
the same to this office as early as practicable.　Should it be
possible to obtain from the municipal authorities a recent
analysis, made under their supervision, of the water referred
to you are also requested to procure and forward a copy of the
same.

　　　　　　　　　　Respectfully,

　　　　　　　　　　　　　　[signature]
　　　　　　　　　　　　Supervising Architect.

Rev Mins,
    Denver, Colorado.

....pt .. ..
... Mar 0 ...., and .. ..
.. ..
... ...

    ... ...

                                    .. ....
                            Supervising A. ...

DENVER, COLORADO: NEW MINT.

In replying to this Letter the initials in upper right-hand corner must be referred to.
(FORWARDING)

The Superintendent of Construction,

United States (new) Mint,

Denver, Colorado.

Sir:

There has been forwarded this day a print
of drawing #69 showing the approaches to the
building under your charge, and I have to request that same be returned to this office at
the earliest date possible, after indicating
thereon the information requested regarding
certain grades and grading.

Respectfully,

Supervising Architect.

R.

Treasury Department

OFFICE OF THE SUPERVISING ARCHITECT

Washington, March 18, 1901.

ret. to photographic views of work on building.

The Superintendent of Repairs,

U. S. Mint Building, (new),

Denver, Colorado.

Sir:

I have the honor to acknowledge the receipt this day of your communication dated Mar.14th, 1901, and to reply to advise you that the matter will receive prompt consideration, and that action will be taken at the earliest possible moment.

Respectfully,

J. KEMPER,

Chief Executive Officer.

struction.

The Superintendent of Construction,

United States New Mint,

Denver, Colorado.

Sir:

I am in receipt of your letter of the 8th
instant in which you state that a quart of the
water to be supplied in connection with the
building under your charge was on that date
forwarded for analysis.

In reply I have to state that this package
has not yet been received, and, in view of the
time which has elapsed since the date of shipment, you are requested to secure and forward
an additional sample at the earliest date practicable.

Respectfully,

Supervising Architect.

1 3 4

Treasury Department,

OFFICE OF THE SUPERVISING ARCHITECT

Washington, March 22,1901.

The Superintendent of Construction,
    U.S.New Mint,
        Denver,Colorado.

Sirs:

    I have the honor to acknowledge the receipt this day of your communication dated March 18, 1901, and in reply to advise you that the matter will receive prompt consideration, and that action will be taken at the earliest possible moment.

        Respectfully,

                J. K. TAYLOR,

                Supervising Architect.

TREASURY DEPARTMENT

OFFICE OF THE SUPERVISING ARCHITECT

Washington, March 23, 1901.

The Superintendent of Construction,

U. S. Mint (New),

Denver, Colorado.

Sir:

Your letter of the 11th instant, reporting progress at
the building under your charge, was duly received, and the
statements made by you noted, in regard to the satisfactory
prosecution of all work under a contract with _____ McIntyre

With reference to your report it appears that upon the
supply of four pieces which have been ordered, to substitute
for broken and defective pieces of material now on hand, this branch of
the work can in a way completed

In submitting your report at the close of this month
please indicate the probable date when, in your judgment, all
work embraced under the contract referred to will be completed

Respectfully,

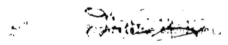

Mee Ellery Bage

    Superintendent Construction

        New Denver Mint,   City.

    Sir,

        Replying to your letter 27th. inst. requesting information as to the date of completion of the Denver Mint (now under my contract, I have the honor to say.

All the Maine granite for the top member of the roof cornice, has been put in place upon the East, North and West sides of the building, and the weather permitting the one on the south side, with the exception of four stone condemned for defects, should be in place by March 30th, inst.

The condemned stone were ordered from the Standard Granite Co. Dec. 29th, 1900 and were again ordered by said Company's agent February 21st, 1901. J. A. Bell the President of said Company advises that it will be impossible to furnish the stone called for before May 1st. nextat which time they will be delivered at the site of the building.

I have already made arrangements to commence April 1st. on the roof tiling and terra cotta partitions, and on the same date to complete the areas and steps.

With the exception of the condemned stone, and that portion of

He must necessarily left open on account of the absence of the
unsigned store, I fully expect, weather permitting, to finish
the building n l later than June 1st. 1901.

I assure you that no effort will be spared to hurry who wish to
completion, and should bad weather not intervene, have every
reason to believe that the building will be completed on the
above have me Dated.

                    Very Respectfully,

The Superintendent of Construction,

United States Assay Mint,

Denver, Colorado.

Sir:

I am in receipt of your letter of the
22nd instant, transmitting a point of drawing
notes for the building under your charge, and
in reply I desire to state that the information therein contained has been noted.

Respectfully,

Supervising Architect

DENVER MINT.

TREASURY DEPARTMENT

OFFICE OF THE SUPERVISING ARCHITECT

Enclosure.

In replying to this Letter the
initials in upper right-hand
corner must be referred to.

Washington, March 29, 1901.

Superintendent of Construction,
        New Mint Building,
            Denver, Colorado.

Sir:-

   I enclose herewith , for your information and the
files of your office, a copy of Department letter of
even date, accepting the proposal-forwarded in your letter
of the 9th instant,- of Mr. J.A.McIntyre, the contractor
for the superstructure, etc. of the building in your
charge, in amount $25.00 to bolt the wood work to the
channel back of roof gutters, as shown on drawing #45,
all as stated in the said letter of acceptance.

   You are hereby authorized to certify and issue vouchers on account of the work, as required by the terms of
the contract and the printed "Instructions to Superintendents," payment of which vouchers the Disbursing A-
gent has been authorized to make from the appropriation
for Mint Building, Denver, Colorado.

                    Respectfully,

                                    Supervising Architect.

J.S.S.

March 30,1901.

Mr. J.A.McIntyre,
    Cooper Building,
        Denver,Colorado.

Fir:-

In view of the statement and recommendation contained in letter of March 9,1901 from the Superintendent of Construction of the new Mint Building in your City, your proposal,dated March 8,1901, addressed to him, in amount twenty-five dollars ($25.00), is hereby accepted to belt the wood work to the channel back of roof gutters, as shown on drawing #45, the same being deemed reasonable, this to be considered as an addition to your contract for the foundation, superstructure, roof covering,etc,of the said building--for which your original proposal was accepted March 20,1898, and a public exigency requiring the immediate performance of the work.

It is understood and agreed that this addition is not to affect the time for the completion of the work as required by the terms of your contract; that the same is without prejudice to any and all rights of the United States thereunder;and without prejudice,also,to any and all rights of the United States against the sureties on the bond executed for the faithful fulfillment of the contract.

Please promptly acknowledge the receipt of this letter, a copy of which will be forwarded to the Superintendent of the building, for his information and guidance.

Respectfully,

J.C.P.   Secretary.

J.R.D.

193

Mr. Henry Moore.

Sec. of Merchants' Association,

Denver, Colorado.

Dear Sir.

In reply to your first advisement this afternoon
I will be pleased if you will advise me of the total number of
cubic feet of lights that are called for in your official estimate,
for use in the United States Mint building under construction.

Yours Respectfully.

TREASURY DEPARTMENT

OFFICE OF THE SUPERVISING ARCHITECT

Washington, **April 2, 1901.**

In replying to this Letter the initials in upper right-hand corner must be referred to.

(ENCLOSURE)

The Superintendent of Construction,

United States (new) Mint,

Denver, Colorado.

Sir:

In reply to your letter of the 26th
ultimo I enclose herewith a pencil sketch
showing the construction and form of the
skylight louvres for the building under
your charge, which sketch will explain the
construction of the louvres more clearly
than shown on drawing #35.

The question of raising the flashing,
as suggested by you, will form the subject
of a separate communication.

Respectfully,

Supervising Architect.

R.

DENVER MINT.

ENCLOSURE.

In replying to this Letter the
initials in upper right-hand
corner must be referred to.

TREASURY DEPARTMENT

OFFICE OF THE SUPERVISING ARCHITECT

Washington,   April 2,1901.

Superintendent of Construction,
    New Mint Building,
        Denver, Colorado.

Sir:-

    Referring to your letter of the 26th ultimo, you are
directed to obtain a proposal for raising flashing about
ventilator of the building in your charge, as indicated on
drawing herewith enclosed, and forward the same to this
Office, as soon as possible, with your definite recommendation.

                    Respectfully,

                              Supervising Architect.

H.M.

DENVER, COLORADO: NEW MINT.

*In replying to this Letter the
initials in upper right-hand
corner must be referred to.*

The Superintendent of Construction,

United States (new) Mint,

Denver, Colorado.

Sir:

The samples of water referred to in
your letter of the 25th ultimo have been
received,but,as the quantity is not sufficient to permit of proper analysis,I
have to request that an additional gallon
be at once forwarded.

I have also to request that you prepare and submit to this office at the
earliest date possible an estimate and
specification for sinking such well,or
wells,as in your judgment may be necessary to furnish an adequate water supply
for the building under your charge.

Respectfully,

Supervising Architect.

R.

Form No. 175.
Ed. 2 1 1901 3,000.

In replying to this Letter the
initials in upper right-hand
corner must be referred to.

Treasury Department,

OFFICE OF THE SUPERVISING ARCHITECT

Washington, April 4, 1901.

The Superintendent of Construction,

    United States (new) Mint,

        Denver, Colorado.

S r:

    I have the honor to acknowledge the receipt this day of your communication dated April 1, 1901, and in reply to advise you that the matter will receive prompt consideration, and that action will be taken at the earliest possible moment.

        Respectfully,

                J. K. TAYLOR,

                Supervising Architect.

Mr Ullery,

Supt. Borough Works,

New York, City.

Dear Sir:-

I have the honor to acknowledge receipt of your letter
April 5th enclosing amended & revised work round daylight manner
and will be pleased to perform said work in accordance therewith

Very respectfully,

S
P

Treasury Department

Washington,   April 8, 1901.

The Superintendent of Construction,

Mint Building, (new),

Denver, Colorado.

In view of your report .... herewith and in

.... of the 3rd instant, and the .... together with

a .... estimate of the expense and performance of .... work you

are hereby authorized to incur an expenditure of eight dol-

lars and fifty-five cents ($8.55)

according to the accompanying .... specification, viz:

water rent for six months from the 1st proximo, $ 6.75

ten (10) gallons of fuel oil   1.80

DENVER, COLO. MINT BLDG.

TREASURY DEPARTMENT

OFFICE OF THE SUPERVISING ARCHITECT

Washington,   April

Superintendent of Construction,
    New Mint Building,
        Denver, Colo.

Sir:

    I have to acknowledge receipt of your letter
的th ultimo to which attention is called that the
stick delivered for the flag pole on the building
change measures only 58 feet in length instead of
as required by the specification, and in which you
that the contractor be allowed to splice on the
8 feet at the bottom in order to avoid the delay
a stick of the required length. You are asked
proposal from the contractor making suitable deduc-
reducing the height of the flag pole 8 feet will

        Respectfully,

              Supervising Architect.

H.M.

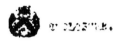

DEPARTMENT

April 15, 1901.

Superintendent of Construction,
New Mint Building,
Denver, Colorado.

I enclose herewith, for your information and the files
your office, a copy of Department letter of even date, ac
ting the proposal of Mr. J. A. McIntyre, in sum of
a balance of $00,000, to additional copper work at source
construction will be eligible to be installed in your
s to be considered as an addition to the contract for the
heating, ventilation etc., duct detecting etc., as a state
condition said letter of acceptance, which explains ther.

You are hereby authorized to certify and issue vouchers
account of the above, as required by the provisions therein
of the Superintendent's signature to the contract, pay
t of and to charge the Disbursing Agent who acts under
the same from the appropriation for New Building, Denver, Col
ado.

Respectfully,

Supervising Architect.

Mr. J. A. McIntyre,
    Cooper Building, Rooms #402-4,
      Denver, Colorado.

Sir:

    In accordance with the statements and recommendation contained in letter of April 10, 1901, from the Superintendent of Construction of the new Mint building at Denver, Colorado, your proposal, dated March 27, 1901, addressed to him, in amount thirty-five dollars ($35.00), is hereby accepted, for additional copper work at louvres in connection with the skylight of said building, as required by the sketch furnished by the Superintendent and to his full satisfaction, the same being deemed reasonable and a public exigency requiring the immediate performance of the work, which is to be considered as an addition to your contract for the foundation, superstructure, roof covering, etc., of the above mentioned building, for which your original proposal was accepted March 29, 1898.

    It is understood and agreed that this addition is not to affect the time fixed for the completion of the entire work in the original contract; that the same is without prejudice to any and all rights of the United States thereunder; and without prejudice, also, to the rights of the United States against the sureties on the bond executed for the faithful performance of the contract.

    Please promptly acknowledge the receipt of this letter.

                   Respectfully,

                                    Secretary.

J.O.F.
E.T.R.

DENVER. New Mint.

TREASURY DEPARTMENT

OFFICE OF THE SUPERVISING ARCHITECT

Washington, April 17,1901.

Superintendent of Construction,

    U.S.Mint (New),

        Denver, Colorado.

Sir:

    Your letter of the 1st instant is acknowledged in relation to the test of terra cotta floor arches at the building under your charge, and the statements made therein are noted.

    In reply, you are advised that it is not the intention to have an Inspector present when the tests are made, and you are requested to give consideration thereto, and to forward for the information of the office pieces of the terra cotta mentioned in your letter as supplied, on which the efflorescence appears, in order that it may be determined whether the same are in accordance with the approved sample.

                Respectfully,

                        Supervising Architect.

TREASURY DEPARTMENT

OFFICE OF THE SUPERVISING ARCHITECT

Washington, April 24, 1901.

Superintendent of Construction,
    New Mint Building,
        Denver, Colorado.

Sir:

I enclose herewith, for your information and the files
of your office, a copy of Department letter of even date, accepting the proposal of Mr. J.A.McIntyre to deduct the sum of
four dollars ($4.00) from the amount to be paid him under his
contract for the foundation, superstructure and roof coverin
of the building in your charge, for which his original proposal was accepted March 29, 1889, on account of being permitted
to erect a flagpole 36'0" long in lieu of the 38'0" flagpole
specified under said contract, all as stated in detail in
said letter of acceptance, which explains itself.

                    Respectfully,

                              Supervising Architect

April 24, 1901.

Mr. J. A. McIntyre,
    Cooper Building, Rooms 402-4,
        Denver, Colorado.

Sir:

In view of the statements and recommendation contained
in letter of April 15, 1901, from the Superintendent of Construction of the New Mint building at Denver, Colorado, your
proposal, dated April 15, 1901, addressed to him, is hereby
accepted, to deduct the sum of four dollars ($4.00) from the
amount to be paid you under your contract dated March 25,1899,
for the foundation, superstructure and roof covering of the
said building, on account of being permitted to erect a 34'4"
long flagpole in lieu of the 35'6" long flagpole specified
under said contract, the amount of the deduction being deemed
reasonable.

It is understood and agreed that this deduction is not
to affect the time for the completion of the entire work as
fixed in the original contract; that the same is without prejudice to any and all rights of the United States thereunder,
and without prejudice, also, to the rights of the United States
against the sureties on the bond executed for the faithful
fulfillment of the contract.

Please promptly acknowledge the receipt of this letter, a
copy of which will be sent to the Superintendent for his information.

                        Respectfully,

                                Secretary.

W.D.
J.A.

Superintendent of Construction,

U. S. Mint (New),

Denver, Colo.

Sir:

Referring to the matter of stone work for the top member of
the main cornice on the building under your charge, and to your
letter of the 16th ultimo in which you state that four new blocks
had been ordered to replace defective pieces, which pieces it is as-
sumed include the two recommended for rejection by Superintendent
Roberts, and the one referred to in your letter of February 21st,
last, as containing a dangerous seam, a letter has been received at
this office from the Standard Granite Company in which they call
attention to defective stones Nos. 16, 66 and 76, and request that
the office permit the use of the same when patched. These three
stones are not identified as having formed the subject of reports
from you, although this may be due to a confusion in the numbers
indicated; and furthermore, it is not shown by the Company named
whether the blocks referred to by them are among the four which
you state have been ordered from Maine to replace defective pieces.

You of course understand that the office , in matters of this
kind, does not deal with sub-contractors, and will not in this case
deal with the firm above named. The conditions reported by them are
submitted to you for your information and appropriate action.

Stone No. 16 they claim has a slight seam which has been tested by throwing it over another block lying immediately under the
seam. The extent or direction of the seam is not shown and the information given is vague and indefinite.

Stone No. 56 they allege has a small piece set in (7"x 2-3/8"
x 1-3/4") and that when the block is set in place the patch will
rest upon and will be completely hidden by the modillion. If this
is as stated by them, it would seem that the stone could be accepted
by you under the general authority conveyed by office telegram and
letter of February 14th, last.

Stone No. 76 they state is on the alley side of the building
and has a small corner broken off, that this small piece which is
not more than 3" x 3" x 2" could be set in the stone without marring
its appearance, and that it will be covered by the copper flashing.
Of course it would be impossible for you, under the authority conveyed by the office on February 14th, last, to accept this stone patched in any manner, as that as patch would be resting on a support
already in place and that it would not be visible. However, it
would seem, if the conditions are as indicated above, that the
stone could be patched by setting in an evenly shaped piece neatly
dressed and dovetailed in a proper manner and laid in melted shellac
or Portland cement colored to match the stone work; or in lieu of
the dovetailing that a brass or heavily galvanized iron dowel be
used. In this manner the patch would be selfsupporting, and if it
is covered by the copper flashing, it is thought that, under the

circumstances, it would be satisfactory.

By these suggestions the office does not wish to bias your judgment in the acceptance or rejection of these stones, which matter is left entirely to you as being more conversant with the local conditions; but it is desired, as far as practicable to expedite matters and secure the completion of the work as early as possible. Referring in this connection to the last paragraph of your letter of February 18th, last, you must be careful, if you accept this stone with the broken corner, not to leave any ground upon which the contractor can base any future claim as suggested.

Respectfully,

Supervising Architect.

920 17th S

Index to letters from

Supervising Architect,
Chief Executive Officer,
&

John A. McIntyre

Chief Executive Officer.

Authority for purchase of photos.
   "   "   "   "   "
   "   "   "   " coal
   "   " water rent
   "   " photos
   "   " coal
   "   " photos
   "   . coal
   "   . bookcase
   "   " photos
   "   " water rent and coal oil